Christine Carlozzi
January 2, 19__

John Clancy's Christmas Cookbook

John Clancy's CHRISTMAS COOKBOOK

HEARST BOOKS · NEW YORK

Acknowledgments:

My special thanks to Launce Blenkin, Russell Carr, Michael Mignone, and Tim Patton, all of whom helped with the preparation of the food that appears in the color sections of this book.

Picture credits:

Festive fruitcakes. Painted tin shapes loaned by Pan American Phoenix, at The Market at Citicorp Center, 153 East 53rd Street, New York, New York 10022.
Breads, simple and fancy. Breads on white tile panel from Country Floors, 300 East 61st Street, New York, New York 10021.
A hearty Christmas breakfast. Pottery plates from Country Floors, 300 East 61st Street, New York, New York 10021.
New Year's day buffet. Bowls from La Cuisiniere, 867 Madison Avenue, New York, New York 10021.
Christmas party fare. Paisley napkins from Frank McIntosh, at Henri Bendel, 10 West 57th Street, New York, New York 10019.
German Christmas dinner. Placemats and napkins from D. Porthault, Incorporated, 57 East 57th Street, New York, New York 10022.

Text design by Jacqueline Schuman
Photography by Richard Jeffery
Styling by Yvonne McHarg
Technique illustrations by Richard Del Rosso

Library of Congress Cataloging in Publication Data
Clancy, John.
    John Clancy's Christmas cookbook.

    Includes index.
    1. Christmas cookery.   I. Title.   II. Title: Christmas cookbook.
TX739.C53   641.5'68   82-6179
ISBN 0-87851-207-1   AACR2

10 9 8 7 6 5 4 3 2 1

Printed in the United States of America

With much love,
for my brother Robert Nicholas
and
my lifelong friend Evelyn Dill Schorske,
who were both born on Christmas Eve

CONTENTS

INTRODUCTION *ix*

PART ONE • Preparing for the Holidays

Mincemeat, Plum Pudding, and Fruitcakes *3*

Cookies *13*

Cakes, Breads, and Tarts *27*

Stocking Stuffers *55*

Canapés and Hors d'Oeuvres *61*

PART TWO • Christmas Menus

Christmas Parties *75*

Brunch *87*

Christmas Eve Buffet *101*

Christmas Day Breakfast *111*

Traditional Dinners *115*

New Year's Eve Buffet *131*

New Year's Day Open House *143*

INDEX *159*

INTRODUCTION

I am unashamedly in love with Christmas. I still vividly remember when I was very young, how I believed in Santa Claus and delighted in the bustle and special aromas associated with my mother's preparation of food for the holidays. With the exception of holiday cooking, Christmas was never visible until Christmas morning. My father decorated the tree and brought out the presents only after we children were tucked in our beds on Christmas Eve. Consequently, waking up to a house that was suddenly full of Christmas was always very exciting. I am also sentimental about, and still use, the tree ornaments my grandparents brought here from Germany at the turn of the century. And although I didn't know I would write a cookbook especially for Christmas when I bought my brownstone home in the Chelsea area of New York City, it seems very appropriate now that I have done so, because the house sits on land once owned by Clement Clarke Moore, the author of *A Visit from St. Nicholas* ("The Night Before Christmas").

Two recent factors actually led me to write this book, however. The first was the popularity of my holiday baking class; the second, the response from readers to a magazine article I wrote about my mother's traditional Thanksgiving menu. Many people told me that they used the article to re-create the same meal, and that it was a helpful guide to follow because it got them easily through an event that had previously proved to be an ordeal. From their experiences I realized that many cooks miss out on the real enjoyment of the holidays because they fail to plan and prepare the food far enough ahead of time. As you read this book you will find that I have stressed the importance of organizing your time and preparing as much food as possible in advance, a strategy that makes for pleasurable and successful entertaining.

The chapter introductions as well as the recipes contain much helpful information to make your entertaining easier. The last six chapters in the book are based on menus that you should find useful both as is and as a source for dishes you can use to devise your own appetizing menus. My special hope is that you will enjoy, as much as my family and friends do, the memorable flavors of Christmas.

John W. Clancy

PART ONE

PREPARING FOR CHRISTMAS

Mincemeat, Plum Pudding, and Fruitcakes

Although many of the dishes in this book may be prepared ahead of time, those in this chapter absolutely *must* be made in advance so their flavor and character will have time to develop fully. For many people, including myself, Christmas memories are associated with this early baking, often a congenial task shared with family and friends. I always like to begin with making the mincemeat that will later fill Christmas tarts and pies. Its aroma alone puts me in a holiday mood and provides the incentive to continue with the fruitcakes and puddings that will eventually be on my holiday table or be presented as gifts. Not only is the scent of mincemeat a pleasure but the broth from making it forms a hearty base for a good cold-weather soup that I can enjoy right away or freeze for use over the holidays.

I begin my advance baking as early as two months before Christmas when dried and candied fruits are at their best. Three weeks ahead of time is fine for the fruitcakes and plum pudding, but a month or two is even better. To mellow truly, the Scotch bun should be made two to three weeks before you intend to serve it. It has been my experience as a cooking teacher that people always love to make things in advance. The pleasure in doing so increases when you know that long before the many last-minute activities of a holiday some of the major work has already been done.

Old-fashioned Dark Fruitcake

One early October Sunday morning five years ago, my good friend Sally Darr, chef and owner of La Tulipe Restaurant in Greenwich Village, arrived at my house. We had set the day aside to bake this delicious fruitcake for our families and friends. To speed our work, I had already purchased all the ingredients and I had macerated the fruit in rum for several days.

Before long, we found ourselves up to our elbows in fruitcake batter, which we then spooned into pans of different sizes to make one-, two-, and five-pound cakes. (We used the aluminum-foil pans that are readily available in most supermarkets.) By five o'clock that afternoon, our labors yielded 110 pounds of fruitcake. The cakes were cooling on every empty surface in the kitchen, dining room, and living room. When they were cool, we wrapped them in cheesecloth and set them aside to age for about 10 weeks. At our next meeting, the cakes received their last sprinkling of spirits and were then decorated, glazed, and gift wrapped.

The recipe given here makes one five-pound cake. However, if you wish, the batter can be divided to make smaller cakes.

Cake

YIELD: ONE 5-POUND CAKE

2 cups white raisins
2 cups dried currants
$\frac{1}{2}$ cup candied lemon
$\frac{1}{2}$ cup candied orange
$\frac{1}{2}$ cup candied citron
1 cup candied cherries
1 cup dry sherry
2 tablespoons, plus $\frac{1}{2}$ pound (2 sticks), unsalted butter, softened
2 tablespoons, plus 2 cups all-purpose flour
$1\frac{1}{2}$ teaspoons double-acting baking powder
$\frac{1}{2}$ teaspoon salt
1 cup dark brown sugar
1 cup ground almonds
4 large eggs

1. Combine the raisins, currants, and all the candied fruit in a large mixing bowl. Pour $\frac{1}{2}$ cup of the sherry over the fruit and stir the fruit with a large spoon until all the pieces are moistened with the sherry. Let the fruit soak overnight, or for several days if possible.

2. Preheat the oven to 325°.

3. Grease the entire inside of a 12-inch springform pan with the 2 tablespoons of softened butter. Sprinkle the pan with the 2 tablespoons of flour. Tilt the pan from side to side to coat it evenly with the flour. Invert the pan and tap it gently to remove any excess flour.

4. Sift the remaining flour, the baking powder, and the salt over the fruit mixture. Now toss the fruit with your fingers until it is completely coated with the dry ingredients.

5. In another bowl, cream the softened $\frac{1}{2}$ pound of butter with the brown sugar until the mixture is light and fluffy. Gradually add the ground almonds, then beat in the eggs,

one at a time, beating well after each addition. Stir in the fruit mixture and blend thoroughly. With a rubber spatula, scrape the cake batter into the prepared pan.

6. Bake on a rack in the middle of the oven for 1 hour and 45 minutes, or until a cake tester inserted into the cake comes out clean. Set the cake on a wire rack and let it cool to room temperature before removing it from the pan.

7. Place a double thickness of cheesecloth on a large, shallow plate. Place the cake right side up on top of the cheesecloth and sprinkle it with the remaining $\frac{1}{2}$ cup of sherry. Wrap the cake in the cloth, then wrap it again in foil or place it in a tin cake box to age at room temperature for about 10 weeks. The cake will keep at room temperature for up to a year if sprinkled lightly with sherry once a month; it will keep indefinitely in the refrigerator.

8. About 2 weeks before serving, remove the cheesecloth, and glaze and decorate the cake following the directions given below.

Glaze and Decoration

*1½ cups apricot preserves
2 tablespoons water
Angelica; candied cherries, cut in half; blanched almonds; walnut or pecan halves, optional*

1. Place the apricot preserves and water in a small saucepan and set the pan over low heat until the preserves melt. Raise the heat and bring the mixture to a boil; be careful not to scorch the preserves. Stir with a wooden spoon until the mixture has reduced to about 1 cup. Push the preserves through a fine sieve into a small bowl.

2. Using a pastry brush, coat the entire surface of the cake with half of the glaze. While the glaze is still warm and soft, apply any decoration of fruit and nuts you wish to add. (See the photograph of fruitcakes in the first color section for ideas.) When the remaining glaze has cooled to room temperature and the decorations have adhered firmly to the cake, glaze the cake again, completely covering the decorations as well. Let the cake sit for several hours until the glaze sets, then wrap it completely in plastic wrap. Store in a tin at room temperature for 2 to 3 weeks, or until ready to use. Refrigerated, the glazed cake will keep for up to a year in this state.

Golden Fruitcake

YIELD: ONE 10-INCH CAKE

1½ cups golden raisins
1 cup diced candied citron
1 cup diced candied orange
1 cup diced candied
    pineapple
1¼ cups dark rum
12 tablespoons butter (1½
    sticks), softened
2 tablespoons, plus 3 cups,
    all-purpose flour
2 teaspoons double-acting
    baking powder
½ teaspoon freshly grated
    nutmeg
¾ teaspoon salt
1 cup granulated sugar
4 large egg yolks
1 cup blanched almonds,
    coarsely chopped
8 large egg whites

1. Combine the raisins and all the candied fruit in a large mixing bowl. Pour one cup of the rum over the fruit and stir until all the pieces are moistened with the rum. Let the fruit soak overnight, or for several days if possible.

2. Preheat the oven to 325°.

3. Grease the entire inside of a 10-inch springform tube pan with 2 tablespoons of the butter. Sprinkle the 2 table-spoons of flour around the pan and tilt the pan from side to side to coat it evenly with the flour. Invert the pan and tap it gently to remove any excess flour.

4. Sift the remaining flour, baking powder, nutmeg, and salt together into a large bowl.

5. In another large bowl, with a large spoon cream the remaining butter with ½ cup of the sugar until the mixture is light and fluffy. Add the egg yolks one at a time, beating well after each addition.

6. Toss the candied fruit and the chopped almonds with the sifted dry ingredients until the fruit and almonds are thoroughly coated. Stir the fruit mixture into the butter mixture.

7. Beat the egg whites until they hold soft peaks when the beater is lifted. Gradually add the remaining ½ cup of sugar and continue beating until the whites hold stiff peaks. Spoon one quarter of the beaten egg whites over the fruit batter and stir them together thoroughly. Then gently fold in the remaining egg whites. Scrape the cake batter into the prepared pan and smooth the top.

8. Bake on a rack in the middle of the oven for 2 hours, or until a cake tester inserted in the center of the cake comes out clean.

9. Let the cake cool to room temperature on a wire rack before removing it from the pan. Lay a double thickness of cheesecloth across a large deep plate. Place the cooled cake on the cheesecloth, and sprinkle the cake evenly with the remaining ¼ cup of rum. Wrap the cake in the cheesecloth and then wrap it in foil or place it in a cake tin. Keep the

cake at room temperature for at least 2 weeks—2 months is even better—before serving or glazing. The cake will actually keep at room temperature for up to a year if sprinkled lightly once a month with rum; it will keep indefinitely in the refrigerator.

10. About 2 weeks before serving, remove the cheesecloth, and glaze and decorate the cake following the directions given for the old-fashioned dark fruitcake, page 5.

Holiday Mincemeat *make in Sept*

Although mincemeat can be used when it is only two weeks old, I prefer making it in the early fall and letting it stand a long time before the holidays; the longer it sits, the richer it gets. To balance its richness, mincemeat should be mixed with equal quantities of fresh apples or pears. Because it will absorb more alcohol than any other food I can think of, mincemeat can be stored at room temperature indefinitely. The first several weeks, check it every five days or so to make sure it looks slightly wet. If it seems dry, add more alcohol. This recipe calls for brandy; however, you may use rum, scotch, bourbon, or a mixture of all four. As James Beard once said, "Making mincemeat is a wonderful way to clean the liquor cabinet."

YIELD: 12 TO 14 CUPS

2 pounds lean brisket of
   beef
2 teaspoons salt
½ pound beef suet
2 cups seedless raisins
2 cups currants
4 cups peeled and chopped
   apples
½ cup diced citron
½ cup diced orange peel
½ cup diced lemon peel
1 cup granulated sugar
1 teaspoon nutmeg
1 teaspoon cinnamon
½ teaspoon allspice
½ teaspoon ground cloves
Brandy or other spirits

1. Place the brisket in a pot just large enough to hold it and cover the meat with water. Bring the water to a boil, add 1 teaspoon of the salt, and reduce the heat to a simmer. Cook the meat for 2½ to 3 hours, or until it can be shredded with two forks. Shred the brisket.

2. With a large knife, finely chop the beef suet and add it to the brisket. (Put a little vegetable oil on the blade to keep the suet from sticking to the knife.)

3. Mix the shredded brisket and all the remaining ingredients, except the brandy, in a large storage crock that has a tight-fitting lid. Then add enough brandy to almost cover the mincemeat. Place the lid on the crock and let the mincemeat stand for at least 2 weeks before using.

Scotch Black Bun

Because of its elegant pastry covering, Scotch black bun, a traditional New Year's Eve offering in Scotland, is one of the most unusual and decorative of all fruitcakes. The black bun pictured in the first color section was made in a French pâté mold I bought many years ago at Elizabeth David's shop in London. The cake can also be made in a springform pan.

YIELD: 16 TO 20 SERVINGS

¾ *pound unsalted butter (3 sticks), chilled and cut into small pieces*
3¾ *cups all-purpose flour, plus 3½ cups all-purpose flour*
½ *teaspoon salt*
8 to 10 *tablespoons ice water*
½ *cup sugar*
½ *teaspoon baking powder*
1 *teaspoon cinnamon*
½ *teaspoon mace*
⅛ *teaspoon allspice*
¼ *teaspoon freshly ground black pepper*
3 *cups seedless raisins*
3 *cups white raisins*
½ *cup blanched almonds, ground*
1½ *cups almonds, coarsely chopped*
3 *large eggs*
½ *cup milk or buttermilk*
1 *cup brandy*
1 *egg, beaten*

1. In a medium-sized mixing bowl, combine the butter, 3¾ cups flour, and ¼ teaspoon of the salt. With your fingers work the ingredients together until you form small granules that are fairly uniform in size. Sprinkle 8 tablespoons of the ice water over the granules and continue mixing until you can gather the ingredients into a ball. If the dough crumbles, add additional ice water, 1 tablespoon at a time, until a soft ball can be formed. With the flat of your hand, press the dough into a thick cake, wrap it in plastic wrap, and refrigerate for 1 hour.

2. Prepare the filling by sifting the 3½ cups flour, sugar, baking powder, cinnamon, mace, allspice, and remaining ¼ teaspoon of salt together into a large bowl. Add the freshly ground black pepper, seedless and white raisins, ground and coarsely chopped almonds. Mix thoroughly until all the fruit and nuts are well coated with the dry ingredients. Add the 3 eggs, milk, and brandy and mix well.

3. Preheat the oven to 375°.

4. On a lightly floured surface, roll two-thirds of the chilled pastry to a thickness of ¼ inch. Gently place a circular 7-by-4-inch pâté mold or a 9-by-3½-inch springform pan on the pastry. With a small knife, cut along the outside of the form to make a disk. Line the bottom of the pan with the disk of pastry. (If you use a pâté mold, place it on a cookie sheet.) Use the remaining pieces of rolled-out pastry to line the sides of the mold or pan, slightly overlapping the pastry on the bottom and letting the pastry extend about ½ inch above the top of the form.

5. Spoon the filling into the pan, packing it down firmly, and press the excess pastry over the filling. Brush the pastry with a little of the beaten egg.

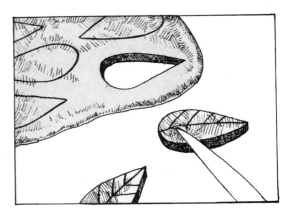

Making pastry leaves. *Using a paring knife, cut pastry leaves that are about 1¼ inches long out of dough that has been rolled to a thickness of ¼ inch. Lift the leaves from the dough with the tip of the knife. Then, using the back of the knife, press a line down the center of each leaf and mark the veins of the leaf on both sides of the line. When applying the leaves to pastry, lift or curl some of the edges to make them look more natural.*

6. In the same fashion, roll the remaining pastry into a circle larger than the form. Roll the pastry around the rolling pin to lift it and unroll it on top of the form. Press the top pastry against the filling and pastry below to make a tight seal, and trim off the excess. Brush the entire top with the beaten egg. Cut a 1-inch round vent in the middle of the bun, and if you like, use the pastry scraps to make leaves (see the first color section and the illustration above) or any decoration of your choice. Brush the underside of the decorations with beaten egg to make them adhere to the top of the bun. Again brush the entire top of the bun and the decorations with beaten egg. Bake on a rack in the middle of the oven for 2 to 2½ hours, or until the pastry is a rich golden brown. If the decorations color much faster than the top sheath of pastry, cover them with aluminum foil to reflect the oven heat and to retard the coloring.

Coach House Plum Pudding

The Coach House Restaurant in New York is a notable four-star establishment to which I have had a long attachment. I can still remember my first visit there in the Spring of 1958, and the exquisite taste of the icy-cold oysters, triple-cut loin lamb chop, and pecan pie that I was served. Little did I know then that I would become chef of the restaurant in a few short years.

One of the best creations served at the Coach House is the greatest plum pudding I have ever tasted, a traditional offering during the Christmas season. Now, thanks to Leon Lianidies, the owner of the restaurant, whose generosity has never been bound to any season, I am able to share the recipe with you. Although the proportions have been scaled to size for family entertaining, the flavor is as wonderful as ever.

Pudding

YIELD: 18 TO 24 SERVINGS

$1\frac{1}{2}$ cups all-purpose flour
1 teaspoon double-acting
    baking powder
$1\frac{1}{2}$ teaspoons salt
4 teaspoons ground ginger
$\frac{1}{2}$ teaspoon freshly grated
    nutmeg
3 cups seedless raisins
3 cups sultana raisins
3 cups muscat raisins
$\frac{1}{4}$ cup candied orange peel
$\frac{1}{4}$ cup candied lemon peel
$\frac{1}{2}$ cup sliced almonds
3 cups fine dry bread
    crumbs
1 pound beef suet, ground
2 cups dark brown sugar
$\frac{1}{2}$ cup brandy
8 large eggs, beaten

1. Sift the flour, baking powder, salt, ground ginger, and grated nutmeg together into a large bowl. Add the sultana and muscat raisins, candied orange and lemon peel, and the almonds, and toss them around with your fingers until they are coated with the seasoned flour. Add the bread crumbs, beef suet, brown sugar, brandy, and beaten eggs, mixing well after each addition. Cover and refrigerate overnight.

2. Line a 10-cup steamed-pudding mold loosely with a double thickness of cheesecloth that is large enough to hang over the top of the mold by about 5 inches. With your hands, pack the pudding into the mold. Fold the edge of the cheesecloth over the pudding, place the lid on the mold, and set the pudding aside.

3. Bring 6 quarts of water to a boil in a 10- to 12-quart saucepan, lower the heat to a simmer, and place the mold in the pan. Cover the pan tightly and let the pudding steam for 10 hours. As the water in the pan cooks away, replenish it with additional water. When the pudding is done, remove it from the water and let it cool overnight before storing it in the mold in the refrigerator. Refrigerated, the pudding will keep for a year.

4. Before serving, steam the pudding again for 2 hours, following the instructions in Step 3. Remove the mold from

the pan and dry it with paper towels. Remove the cover from the mold and lift the cheesecloth from the top of the pudding. Place an inverted serving plate over the top of the mold and, with both hands, hold the plate and mold together tightly; turn them over and lift the mold from the pudding. Remove the cheesecloth and let the pudding cool to room temperature before glazing it.

Glaze

1 cup apricot preserves

Place the apricot preserves in a small saucepan and warm over low heat until the preserve melts. Push the preserves through a fine sieve into a small bowl and, using a pastry brush, coat the entire surface of the plum pudding with the glaze. If you want to be traditional, decorate the top of the pudding with a sprig of holly. The English also like to flame the pudding with brandy when presenting it. If you wish to follow suit, omit the glaze and heat $\frac{1}{4}$ cup brandy in a small saucepan, pour it over the pudding, and light it immediately.

Hard Sauce

8 tablespoons (1 stick)
  unsalted butter
$\frac{1}{2}$ cup granulated sugar
$\frac{1}{4}$ cup brandy
$\frac{1}{2}$ teaspoon vanilla extract

Place all of the ingredients in the bowl of an electric mixer and cream them together until smooth. Refrigerate until slightly firm. Shape the chilled hard sauce mixture into a cylinder about 7 inches long. Wrap it in wax paper and return it to the refrigerator. To serve, slice the hard sauce into $\frac{1}{3}$-inch-thick rounds and place a round on each slice of the plum pudding.

Cookies

Christmas cookies have a very special meaning for me. When I was a young man, I baked 750 cookies one Sunday afternoon in preparation for our family Christmas. Although, I have to admit, I wasn't eager to bake another cookie very soon, the accomplishment helped me to decide I wanted to be in the food business. The number of cookies you want to make may be more modest, but you will still find it helpful that all of the cookie dough in the following recipes, with the exception of the wasps' nests, can be frozen successfully. This means you can start making the cookie dough in October, saving the shaping, baking, and decorating for later. The dough for freezing should be wrapped well in freezer paper and then placed with identification tags in plastic bags. The night before you intend to roll out the dough, transfer it from the freezer to the refrigerator to thaw. Bear in mind to begin your baking with the cookies that will keep the longest after they come out of the oven. Stored in closed containers, springerle, pfeffernusse, anise cookies, and spiced Christmas trees will all taste fine for a couple of weeks. Cookies such as spritz, Evelyn's Christmas cookies, and the almond crescents should be baked shortly before you want them on hand.

Homemade cookies make wonderful gifts, and all colors and sizes of imported tin boxes are available around holiday time for use as containers. My mother used to buy apothecary jars, fill them with cookies and decorate the jars with ribbons. A more inexpensive way to present cookies, is to cut out eight- or ten-inch heavy cardboard disks or buy layer cake disks from your local baker. Then, using the disk as a tray for the cookies, wrap it beanbag fashion in bright-colored cellophane and secure the top with a ribbon. For some people on your list, you might want to accompany the cookies with unusual cookie cutters, a springerle board, and/or the recipe itself printed on a gift card.

Lebkuchen

Next to marzipan, *lebkuchen* are probably the most popular and artistic confections in Germany. A specialty of Nuremberg, *lebkuchen* can be found at Christmas time in many holiday shapes, including those of Santas, gingerbread men, stars, and animals, just to mention a few. Not reserved for Christmas alone, however, *lebkuchen* are also made to celebrate many holidays throughout the year, when they take on many other forms. They are sold at carnivals and market places in varying sizes, ranging from small cookies to large plaques bearing inscriptions and decorations in gaily colored icing. Whichever shapes you choose to make, these spicy treats will keep for several months in an airtight container.

YIELD: 3 DOZEN COOKIES

2 tablespoons butter,
   softened
2 tablespoons, plus $2\frac{1}{2}$
   cups, all-purpose flour
$\frac{3}{4}$ teaspoon baking powder
$\frac{1}{2}$ teaspoon ground cloves
1 teaspoon ground
   cinnamon
$\frac{1}{4}$ teaspoon ground nutmeg
1 cup unblanched almonds,
   ground
2 tablespoons candied
   citron, finely chopped
2 tablespoons candied
   lemon, finely chopped
2 tablespoons candied
   orange, finely chopped
2 eggs
$\frac{1}{2}$ cup granulated sugar
$\frac{1}{2}$ cup honey
$\frac{1}{2}$ cup milk

Cookies

1. Grease a $17\frac{1}{2}$-by-$11\frac{1}{2}$-inch jelly-roll pan with the softened butter. Sprinkle the pan with the 2 tablespoons of flour and tilt the pan from side to side to coat it evenly with flour.

2. Preheat the oven to 400°.

3. Sift the remaining $2\frac{1}{4}$ cups of flour, baking powder, cloves, cinnamon, and nutmeg into a large bowl. Add the ground almonds and finely chopped candied fruits and set aside.

4. Beat the eggs with the sugar until thick and very light in color. Stir in the honey, milk, and flour mixture and continue stirring until all the ingredients are well blended. Spread the cookie dough out evenly in the prepared pan. Bake on the middle rack of the oven for 12 minutes, or until the cake is firm to the touch.

5. With two large spatulas, lift the cake out of the pan onto a wire rack and, while it is still warm, brush it with the glaze. Let the glaze set for 3 to 4 minutes, then transfer the cake to a flat surface and cut it into $2\frac{1}{2}$-by-$1\frac{1}{2}$-inch cookies. If you wish to use cookie cutters and apply the icing in special patterns, let the cake cool on a rack for a few minutes, then cut it into various shapes and apply the icing as desired with a watercolor brush. For more colorful effects, you may also tint the icing with vegetable coloring and apply colored sugar in various designs to the wet icing.

Almond Glaze

1 cup confectioners' sugar
¼ teaspoon almond extract
1 teaspoon fresh lemon
   juice
2 tablespoons water

To make the glaze, sift the confectioners' sugar into a small bowl. Add the almond extract, lemon juice, and water, and beat with a wire whisk until the mixture turns into a smooth, thin glaze. Add additional water if necessary. Cover with a damp kitchen towel or plastic wrap until ready to use to keep a crust from forming on the glaze.

Pfeffernusse

Anne Lanigan, a good friend and author of *The Cookie and Cracker Cookbook,* has kindly shared this recipe with me.

YIELD: ABOUT 4 DOZEN
COOKIES

1½ cups sifted all-purpose
   flour
½ teaspoon ground
   cinnamon
¼ teaspoon ground cloves
Pinch ground cardamon
Pinch freshly ground white
   pepper
2 large eggs
½ cup granulated sugar
3 tablespoons blanched
   almonds, finely chopped
1½ teaspoons candied
   citron, finely chopped
1½ teaspoons candied
   orange peel, finely
   chopped
½ teaspoon freshly grated
   lemon rind
Confectioners' sugar

1. Resift the flour with the cinnamon, cloves, cardamon, and white pepper.

2. Beat the eggs and sugar until thick and very light in color. Gradually beat in the flour mixture, almonds, citron, orange peel, and grated lemon rind. Continue to beat until the ingredients are thoroughly incorporated. Form the dough into a ball, wrap it with plastic wrap, and refrigerate for 2 to 3 days.

3. Lightly butter and flour two cookie sheets.

4. Preheat the oven to 325°.

5. Remove the dough from the refrigerator and roll it into a 1-inch-thick cylinder. Slice the dough into ½-inch-thick rounds and place them 1 inch apart on the prepared cookie sheets. Bake the cookies, one sheet at a time, on a rack in the middle oven for 15 to 18 minutes, or until light brown in color. Transfer them to wire racks to cool.

6. Store the cookies together with half an apple in an airtight container for 1 to 2 weeks before eating. (The moisture of the apple will keep the cookies from getting too hard.) Dust with confectioners' sugar before serving.

Spiced Christmas Trees

YIELD: 2 DOZEN 3-BY-4-INCH
COOKIES

½ pound (2 sticks) unsalted
  butter
1 cup granulated sugar
1 large egg
½ cup honey
4½ cups all-purpose flour
¾ teaspoon double-acting
  baking powder
½ teaspoon salt
2 teaspoons ground ginger
1 teaspoon ground
  cinnamon

1. Cream the butter and sugar together until very light in color. Add the egg and honey and continue to beat the mixture until it is light and fluffy.

2. Sift the flour, baking powder, salt, ground ginger, ground cloves, and cinnamon together, and stir into the butter mixture.

3. Wrap the cookie dough in wax paper and chill in the refrigerator for 1 hour.

4. Preheat the oven to 375°.

5. Roll the chilled dough until it is ⅛-inch thick and cut it with a Christmas-tree-shaped cookie cutter. Place the cookies on a lightly greased baking sheet and, if you like, sprinkle them with multi-colored sugar.

6. Bake on a rack in the middle of the oven for about 12 minutes, or until the cookies are slightly firm.

Wasps' Nests

YIELD: 3 DOZEN COOKIES

2 large egg whites
½ cup granulated sugar
¼ teaspoon vanilla extract
Pinch ground cinnamon
Pinch ground cloves
2 ounces semisweet
  chocolate, coarsely
  chopped
1 cup slivered almonds,
  toasted

1. Preheat the oven to 350°.

2. Lightly butter and flour one or two cookie sheets.

3. In a medium-sized bowl, beat the egg whites until they form soft peaks when the beater is lifted. Gradually add the sugar, then the vanilla, cinnamon, and cloves. Continue to beat the mixture until the egg whites hold firm peaks, then fold in the chopped chocolate and the toasted almonds.

4. To shape each cookie, form a bit of dough between 2 teaspoons and set it on the cookie sheet. Space the cookies about 1½ inches apart. Bake the cookies, one sheet at a time, on a rack in the middle of the oven for 12 to 15 minutes, or until the cookies are light gray in color.

Spiced Mushroom Cookies

Mushrooms

YIELD: 3 DOZEN COOKIES

4 tablespoons unsalted
   butter
½ cup granulated sugar
2 large eggs
¼ cup sour cream
¾ cup honey
4 cups all-purpose flour
1½ teaspoons baking soda
1 teaspoon ground
   cinnamon
¼ teaspoon ground allspice
¼ teaspoon freshly grated
   nutmeg
½ teaspoon ground ginger
½ teaspoon freshly grated
   lemon rind

1. Cream the butter and sugar together until they are very light in color. Add the eggs, one at a time, beating well after each addition. Stir in the sour cream and honey.

2. Sift the flour, baking soda, cinnamon, allspice, nutmeg, and ginger together. Add the lemon rind. Stir the flour mixture into the honey mixture to form a soft dough. Wrap the dough in wax paper and chill it in the refrigerator for 1 hour.

3. Preheat the oven to 375°.

4. Lightly grease a baking sheet. To form each mushroom cap, pat about 1½ tablespoons of the dough at a time into a ball. Then dip a fingertip into the flour and press it into the ball. Place the resulting cap indented side down on the baking sheet. To shape each mushroom stem, roll 1½ tablespoons of the dough between your palms, slightly tapering one end. Place the stems on the baking sheet.

5. Bake the mushroom pieces on a rack in the middle of the oven for 10 to 12 minutes, or until lightly firm to the touch. Transfer them to a wire rack to cool.

Icing

3 cups confectioners' sugar
⅔ cup water
4 teaspoons lemon juice
4 teaspoons unsweetened
   cocoa

1. To make the icing, place the sugar in a large bowl and gradually add the water and lemon juice, beating with a wire whisk to make a thin mixture.

2. One by one, dip the mushroom stems into the icing, coating them evenly. Insert the tapered end of the stem into the underside of a mushroom cap and place the mushroom, stem end up, on wax paper to dry.

3. Whisk the cocoa into the remaining icing. When the stems are dry, dip the mushroom caps into the cocoa icing and gently place them on their sides on the wax paper to dry.

Evelyn's Christmas Cookies

In 1936, on the first morning we were in our new summer house on Long Island, our neighbors, the Dills, came over with their daughter Evelyn to welcome my parents with pots of freshly brewed coffee. It was the start of a beautiful friendship that Evelyn and I are still enjoying and have cherished for more than 46 years. I first tasted these cookies of hers almost 30 years ago and I can't remember how many hundreds I must have consumed since then.

YIELD: 4 DOZEN COOKIES

$\frac{1}{2}$ pound unsalted butter (2 sticks)
$\frac{2}{3}$ cup granulated sugar
2 large egg yolks
2 teaspoons vanilla extract
2 cups all-purpose flour, sifted
$\frac{1}{2}$ cup currant jelly

1. Preheat the oven to 375°.

2. Cream the butter and sugar until very light in color. Add the egg yolks and continue to beat until the mixture is fluffy. Stir in the vanilla, and gradually add the flour.

3. To form the cookies, pat 1 tablespoon of dough at a time into a 1-inch-diameter ball and place it on a lightly greased baking sheet. With your fingertip, make an indentation in the top of each cookie. Spoon currant jelly into each indentation.

4. Bake the cookies on the middle rack of the oven for about 8 minutes, or until the edges turn a light golden brown.

Almond Crescents

YIELD: ABOUT 3 DOZEN COOKIES

$\frac{1}{2}$ pound unsalted butter (2 sticks), softened
$\frac{2}{3}$ cup granulated sugar
2 cups all-purpose flour
$1\frac{1}{4}$ cups blanched almonds, ground
1 teaspoon vanilla extract
$\frac{1}{2}$ teaspoon salt
$\frac{3}{4}$ cup confectioners' sugar

1. Cream the butter and sugar together until very light in color. Sift in the flour, $\frac{1}{2}$ cup at a time, mixing well after each addition. Stir in the nuts, vanilla extract, and salt, and continue mixing until the ingredients are well blended. Shape the cookie dough into a ball, wrap it in plastic wrap, and refrigerate for 1 hour.

2. Preheat the oven to 350°

3. Lightly butter and flour two cookie sheets.

4. For each cookie, pinch off enough dough to make a ball about $1\frac{1}{4}$ inches in diameter. Shape each cookie by rolling

the ball between the palms of your hands into a strip about $\frac{1}{2}$ inch thick with slightly tapered ends. Place the strips on the prepared cookie sheets, and shape them into crescents.

5. Bake the cookies, one sheet at a time, on a rack in the middle of the oven for 15 to 20 minutes, or until light gold in color.

6. Let the cookies cool on the baking sheet for a few minutes before transferring them to a wire rack to cool. Sift the confectioners' sugar over them while they are still slightly warm.

Spritz Cookies

If you wish, you may double or quadruple this recipe, then divide the dough into three or four small bowls and, using pure extracts, flavor each batch differently. Cookies flavored with anise should be stored separately, however, because the intense flavor of the spice tends to permeate other foods. You may also flavor the dough with lemon or orange rind, grated finely enough so it won't clog the cookie press or star tube. After shaping the cookies on the cookie sheet, decorate them with bits of candied fruit, angelica, nuts, or a sprinkling of colored sugar.

YIELD: 3 DOZEN COOKIES

$\frac{1}{2}$ pound unsalted butter (2 sticks)
$\frac{2}{3}$ cup granulated sugar
4 large egg yolks
2 cups flour, sifted
$\frac{1}{8}$ teaspoon salt
$1\frac{1}{2}$ teaspoons vanilla extract

1. Preheat the oven to 375°.

2. In a large mixing bowl, cream the butter and sugar together until they are very light in color. Add the egg yolks one at a time, scraping the bottom and sides of the bowl after each addition. Add the flour, salt, and vanilla extract, and mix all the ingredients until well blended.

3. Force the cookie dough through a press or a pastry bag fitted with a number 4 or 5 star tube onto a cookie sheet, making the cookies about $1\frac{1}{4}$ inches across and spacing them about $1\frac{1}{2}$ inches apart.

4. Bake the cookies on a rack in the middle of the oven for 8 to 10 minutes, or until they are lightly browned.

Walnut Balls

YIELD: 3 DOZEN COOKIES

$\frac{1}{2}$ *pound unsalted butter (2 sticks), melted and cooled to room temperature*
3 tablespoons, plus $\frac{3}{4}$ cup, confectioners' sugar
1 teaspoon double-acting baking powder
$\frac{1}{2}$ *teaspoon salt*
$2\frac{1}{4}$ *cups all-purpose flour*
1 cup finely ground walnuts, or substitute pecans

1. Preheat the oven to 350°.

2. In a large mixing bowl, combine the butter, the 3 table-spoons of confectioners' sugar, baking powder, and salt. Sift in the flour, about $\frac{1}{2}$ cup at a time, mixing well after each addition. Stir in the ground nuts and continue to mix until all the ingredients are well blended.

3. Lightly butter and flour one or two cookie sheets.

4. To form the cookies, pat 1 tablespoon of dough at a time into a 1-inch-diameter ball and place it on a cookie sheet; space the balls about 1 inch apart.

5. Bake the cookies, one sheet at a time, on a rack in the middle of the oven for about 12 minutes, or until they are a light sand color. Transfer the cookies to a wire rack to cool.

6. Sift the remaining $\frac{3}{4}$ cup of confectioners' sugar over the cookies.

Anise Cookies

YIELD: ABOUT 2 DOZEN COOKIES

2 large eggs
$\frac{3}{4}$ *cup granulated sugar*
$1\frac{1}{2}$ *cups all-purpose flour*
$\frac{1}{4}$ *teaspoon double-acting baking powder*
1 teaspoon anise seeds, crushed

1. Lightly butter and flour a cookie sheet.

2. In a large bowl, beat the eggs, then gradually add the sugar and continue beating until the mixture is very thick and light in color.

3. Sift the flour and baking powder together. Gently fold them into the egg mixture one third at a time. Fold in the crushed anise seeds.

4. Spoon the cookie batter in drops about the size of a quarter onto the prepared cookie sheet. Let the cookies stand at room temperature overnight.

5. Preheat the oven to 350°.

6. Bake the cookies on a rack in the middle of the oven for 10 to 12 minutes, or until they are firm and barely turn a pale gold color.

Hazelnut Cookies

YIELD: ABOUT 3 DOZEN
COOKIES

4 large egg whites
1 cup granulated sugar
1 tablespoon lemon juice
1 teaspoon vanilla extract
1¾ cups ground hazelnuts
36 whole hazelnuts

1. Preheat the oven to 350°.

2. Lightly butter and flour two cookie sheets.

3. Beat the egg whites to soft peaks. Gradually add the sugar and continue to beat until the egg whites form a stiff meringue. Beat in the lemon juice and vanilla extract.

4. Place about ¾ cup of the meringue mixture in a small bowl and set aside. Fold the ground hazelnuts into the remaining meringue.

5. To shape the cookies, drop about 1 heaping teaspoon of the nut meringue at a time onto the prepared cookie sheets, leaving 1½ inches between them so they can spread slightly. Spoon a little of the reserved meringue onto each cookie and top it with a whole hazelnut.

6. Bake the cookies, 1 sheet at a time, on a rack in the middle of the oven for 12 to 15 minutes, or until light brown in color. Allow the cookies to cool on the baking sheets for a few minutes before transferring them to wire racks to cool.

Jeanne Clancy's Nut Balls

YIELD: ABOUT 3 DOZEN
COOKIES

8 tablespoons unsalted
   butter (1 stick), softened
¼ cup confectioners' sugar
1 teaspoon vanilla extract
¼ teaspoon salt
1 cup all-purpose flour
1 cup blanched almonds,
   ground
1 large egg, beaten
½ cup pecans, finely
   chopped
18 candied cherries, cut in
   half

1. Preheat the oven to 350°.

2. In a large mixing bowl, cream the butter and sugar together until very light in color. Add the vanilla extract, salt, and ground almonds, and mix well.

3. Pat 1 tablespoon of dough at a time into a 1-inch-diameter ball. Dip each ball into the beaten egg and then roll it in the chopped pecans. Place the nut balls on a lightly buttered cookie sheet and press a cherry half into each one. Bake on a rack in the middle of the oven for 15 minutes. Transfer the cookies to a rack to cool.

Moravian Cutouts

Cookies

YIELD: 2 DOZEN 4-INCH
COOKIES

$\frac{1}{2}$ *pound unsalted butter*
$1\frac{1}{2}$ *cups granulated sugar*
2 *large eggs*
2 *teaspoons vanilla extract,*
   or flavor of your choice
$3\frac{3}{4}$ *cups all-purpose flour,*
   sifted
3 *teaspoons double-acting*
   baking powder
$\frac{1}{2}$ *teaspoon salt*

1. Cream the butter and sugar together until very light in color. Add the eggs, one at a time, and continue to beat until the mixture is light and fluffy. Add the vanilla extract or flavor of your choice.

2. Sift the flour, baking powder, and salt together, and stir into the butter mixture. Wrap the cookie dough in wax paper and chill it in the refrigerator for 1 hour.

3. Preheat the oven to 375°.

4. Roll the chilled dough until it is $\frac{1}{8}$ inch thick and, using cookie cutters, cut it into various shapes, such as toy soldiers, stars, and fish. Place the cookies on a lightly buttered cookie sheet and bake on a rack in the middle of the oven for about 8 minutes, or until they are a light golden brown.

Royal Icing

2 *egg whites*
1 *teaspoon lemon juice*
2 *cups confectioners' sugar,*
   approximately, sifted

In a large bowl, beat the egg whites and lemon juice together with a whisk. Gradually beat in the sugar, until the icing reaches spreading consistency (test it with a spatula or a small watercolor brush). If desired, tint the icing with food coloring and brush or spread it over the cooled cookies in the design of your choice. If you prefer to pipe the icing, add more sugar until it reaches the proper consistency, and apply it with a paper cone made following the instructions given in the recipe for the Christmas log, page 38. While you are working, keep a damp towel over any icing exposed to the air to keep a crust from forming on the top.

A preferred holiday drink. *Frothy holiday eggnog with a* ▶
sprinkling of freshly grated orange rind and nutmeg, and,
in the background, a golden fruitcake.

Breads, simple and fancy. *From top left,
clockwise: loaves of old-fashioned whole
wheat and white bread, German butter
cake, brioche with currants and nuts, plain
brioche, stollen, and a poppy seed wreath*

Refreshing hors d'oeuvres. *From left to right: onion drums, mushrooms stuffed with curried chicken, endive leaves filled with onion-flavored cream cheese and caviar, cucumber boats with shrimp, waffled celery root slices topped with crabmeat, and calamat olives (in the basket)*

Facing page: Festive fruitcakes. *Top to bottom: golden fruitcake, Scotch black bun, and old-fashioned dark fruitcake*

Perfect Christmas presents. *From lower left, clockwise: chocolate truffles, spiced mushroom cookies, Jeanne Clancy's nut balls, irresistible pecans, assorted cookies (St. Nicholas spice cookies, topped with slivered almonds; spritz cookies topped with angelica or pecans; Evelyn's Christmas cookies, with jelly centers; and anise cookies) gingerbread bars and caramel-coated popcorn balls, assorted cookies (in glass jar) marzipan fruit and vegetables, assorted cookies (in glass jar), walnut balls, springerle, and Moravian cutouts*

St. Nicholas Spice Cookies

These cookies are known as *spekulatius* in Germany, *speculaasjes* in Denmark, and *speckulaas* in Holland. All of these countries, plus Belgium, claim them for their own. Whatever their origin, the cookies are enormously popular at Christmas time. Like springerle cookies, St. Nicholas cookies are traditionally printed with molds of animal and human form, as well as with other Christmas designs. If you don't have a special board for the cookies, and want to print them with a design, a springerle board will do just as well. Or simply make plain nut-topped cookies, as described below.

<u>YIELD: 3 DOZEN COOKIES</u>

$\frac{2}{3}$ *cup unsalted butter*
$\frac{1}{2}$ *cup brown sugar*
1$\frac{1}{4}$ cups all-purpose flour
1$\frac{1}{2}$ teaspoons ground cinnamon
$\frac{1}{4}$ *teaspoon ground mace*
$\frac{1}{4}$ *teaspoon ground anise*
Pinch ground ginger
Pinch ground nutmeg
$\frac{1}{4}$ *teaspoon double-acting baking powder*
Pinch salt
2 tablespoons milk
1 cup sliced almonds

1. Cream the butter and sugar together until very light in color. Beat in the milk and set the mixture aside.

2. Sift the flour, cinnamon, mace, anise, ginger, nutmeg, baking powder, and salt together, and stir into the butter mixture. Wrap the cookie dough in wax paper and chill in the refrigerator for 1 hour.

3. Preheat the oven to 350°.

4. Roll the cookie dough into a $\frac{1}{16}$-inch-thick rectangle, and cut the dough into 1$\frac{1}{2}$-by-2$\frac{1}{2}$-inch rectangles or, if you have a springerle board use it to press designs in the dough, and then cut the cookies apart. Transfer the cookies to a lightly buttered baking sheet, brush the tops with milk, and gently press the sliced almonds into the cookies.

5. Bake on a rack in the middle of the oven for 10 to 12 minutes, or until the cookies are firm to the touch.

◄ Yuletide desserts. *From top left, clockwise: walnut layer cake with marzipan nutshells and leaves, Coach House plum pudding, meringue mushrooms, Christmas log, rich mince tartlets, star of Zurich, and cranberry mousse*

Springerle

These elegant embossed cookies originated in the German duchy of Swabia centuries ago. The name springerle is derived from the German word for vaulting horse, which at one time was one of the most popular designs used to decorate the cookies.

If you like browsing through antique shops, you are apt to chance upon large springerle boards with elaborate designs or figures of people or animals. A friend of mine is the happy owner of a 10-by-16-inch springerle board carved with the design of a large rooster. When beautifully painted in detail, using a water color brush and vegetable coloring, such large springerle cookies make exceptional gifts. New springerle boards and rolling pins, either imported or domestically made, can be found in department stores or in housewares specialty shops. However, the domestic ones are usually much smaller and simpler in design.

If you wish, the cookies can also be made into Christmas ornaments. Stick the wide end of a toothpick at the top of each cookie before baking. Remove the toothpick while the cookie is still warm and, when it cools to room temperature, thread a decorative string through the hole and hang the cookie on the Christmas tree.

YIELD: 3 DOZEN 1-BY-2-INCH COOKIES

2 tablespoons butter, softened
1 cup anise seeds
3 large eggs
$1\frac{1}{2}$ cups granulated sugar
1 teaspoon grated lemon rind
3 to $3\frac{1}{2}$ cups all-purpose flour

1. Grease two large baking sheets with the softened butter and sprinkle the sheets with the anise seeds.

2. In a large bowl, beat the eggs. Gradually add the sugar and continue beating until the mixture is very thick and light in color. Beat in the lemon rind. Sift the flour into the egg mixture, 1 cup at a time, and continue beating until you have a medium-firm dough. Remove the dough from the bowl, and place it on a lightly floured surface.

3. Knead the dough by pushing it forward and folding it back in half on top of itself. Continue to knead the dough for about 10 minutes, or until it is smooth. When necessary, sprinkle the dough with enough flour to keep it from sticking to your hands or the work surface. Divide the dough in half and roll each half into a rectangle about $\frac{1}{3}$ inch thick; dust the rolled dough lightly with flour.

4. Using a springerle rolling pin or flat springerle cookie molds, roll or press the cookie designs into the dough. Cut the cookies apart with a sharp knife and place them on the prepared baking sheets. Let the cookies stand at room tem-

perature for 24 hours so the designs will set. With a pastry brush, remove any excess flour from the tops of the cookies before baking.

5. Preheat the oven to 250°.

6. Bake the cookies for 15 to 20 minutes on the middle rack of the oven until they are firm. They should have just a hint of golden color.

Lucia Gingersnaps

Mimi Sheraton is a brilliant food writer and critic, and the author of *Visions of Sugar Plums,* an excellent book on Christmas sweets from many different countries. She claims that these Swedish gingersnaps are among the best cookies she has ever tasted, and has generously consented to let me include the recipe in this book.

YIELD: ABOUT 5 DOZEN
COOKIES

1½ cups heavy cream,
    chilled
2½ cups brown sugar
¾ cup molasses
½ cup dark corn syrup
1 tablespoon ground ginger
4 teaspoons grated lemon
    rind
2 tablespoons baking soda
8 to 9 cups all-purpose
    flour

1. Whip the cream until almost stiff.

2. Combine the sugar, molasses, corn syrup, ginger, lemon rind, and baking soda in a bowl and mix thoroughly.

3. Pour the sugar mixture into the cream and beat with a wooden spoon for 10 minutes. Gradually add 5 cups of the flour and blend thoroughly. Continue adding additional flour until the dough is just smooth enough to handle but still soft and pliable. Wrap in plastic wrap and chill in the refrigerator for several hours or overnight.

4. Preheat the oven to 275°.

5. Lightly butter and flour two cookie sheets.

6. On a lightly floured surface roll the dough out to a thickness of ¼ inch. Using fancy cookie cutters about 2½ inches across, cut out shapes and place them on the prepared baking sheets. Bake the cookies, 1 sheet at a time, on a rack in the middle of the oven for about 12 minutes, or until the cookies are an even golden brown. Transfer them to wire racks to cool.

7. When cool, decorate the cookies with royal icing (see Moravian Cutouts, page 22).

Cakes, Breads, and Tarts

I can't think of any country that doesn't have one or two pastries or breads that are symbolic of special holiday occasions. Besides being so popular, holiday baking seems to be the most creative form of culinary art. Among the recipes that follow are examples of that artistry as it is used to celebrate Christmas in six different countries. Although some of these traditional holiday recipes call for a particular kind of decoration, it is not necessary for you to duplicate every detail. Being flexible is part of the fun. You may want to use your imagination to create variations of your own or you may want to simplify the finishing touches. For instance, the French Christmas log would still be impressive, even if not adorned with meringue mushrooms. The Swiss star of Zurich cake can be completely covered with whipped cream and topped with toasted coconut instead of candied fruit. And for the traditional French king's cake, you can use the traditional New Orleans carnival colors, vary them, or keep the cake a plain snowy white. If the little molds to make the marzipan walnut shells for the walnut cake are not easily available, shelled walnuts alone will do fine.

In addition to dessert confections, the recipes include festive breakfast cakes, such as the German stollen, the Italian panetonne, and the poppy seed wreath (you may substitute sesame seeds if you like). There are also recipes for simple white and whole wheat breads. Even if you seldom bake, I think you will find that there is nothing more gratifying than homemade bread during the holidays. Whether it is plain or fancy, what is important is that you are happy with what you are serving and that it expresses your own holiday spirit.

Brioche

1 package active dry yeast
Pinch, plus $\frac{1}{4}$ cup,
   granulated sugar
$\frac{1}{4}$ cup milk, brought to a
   boil and cooled to
   lukewarm (110° to 115°)
$2\frac{1}{2}$ cups all-purpose flour
$\frac{3}{4}$ teaspoon salt
12 tablespoons unsalted
   butter ($1\frac{1}{2}$ sticks), plus 3
   tablespoons butter,
   softened
3 large eggs, beaten

1. Stir the yeast and a pinch of the sugar into the lukewarm milk. Let the mixture stand until it foams, about 4 to 6 minutes.

2. Place $\frac{1}{2}$ cup of the flour in a medium-sized bowl and add the yeast mixture. Stir together until the milk is absorbed by the flour. Transfer this sponge to your work surface and wash and dry the bowl. Return the sponge to the bowl and cover it with the remaining 2 cups flour. Let the sponge rise for 1 hour.

3. With a wooden spoon, beat the remaining $\frac{1}{4}$ cup of sugar, salt, and the 3 eggs into the sponge and dry flour. Beat in the 12 tablespoons of butter, 3 to 4 tablespoons at a time, until it is well incorporated. Cover with a towel and let the dough rise until it has tripled in size, about 3 hours.

4. With a wooden spoon, stir the dough down, cover with plastic wrap, and refrigerate for 2 hours. Stir the dough down, cover it again, and chill it overnight.

5. Grease 12 small brioche tins with the 3 tablespoons of softened butter.

6. For each brioche, pinch off enough dough to make a ball that will fill a tin by one third. With a lightly floured fingertip, make an indentation through the center of each ball to the bottom of the tin. Divide the remaining dough into 12 uniform balls. One at a time, shape each ball into a cone and insert the pointed end into the cavity of each of the brioches.

7. When all the brioches have received a cone, brush the entire surface with the beaten egg, without letting the egg drip onto the side of the tin. Reserve the beaten egg. Place the tins on a cookie sheet, and let the brioches rise until triple in size, about 3 hours.

8. Preheat the oven to 375°.

9. Brush the brioches again with beaten egg and set the cookie sheet on a rack in the middle of the oven for 14 to 17 minutes, or until the brioches are a deep golden brown.

Brioche Breakfast Cake

2 packages active dry yeast
$\frac{1}{4}$ teaspoon, plus $\frac{1}{2}$ cup,
    granulated sugar
$\frac{1}{2}$ cup milk, brought to a
    boil and cooled to
    lukewarm (110° to 115°)
5 cups all-purpose flour
$1\frac{1}{2}$ teaspoons salt
6 large eggs
$\frac{3}{4}$ pound unsalted butter (3
    sticks), softened
1 egg white, beaten lightly
1 cup walnuts, chopped
$1\frac{1}{4}$ cup currants, soaked in
    boiling water or hot rum
    for 10 minutes and
    patted dry with paper
    towels
$\frac{1}{2}$ cup granulated sugar
2 teaspoons cinnamon

1. Stir the yeast and $\frac{1}{4}$ teaspoon of sugar into the lukewarm milk. Let the mixture stand until it foams, about 4 to 6 minutes.

2. Place 1 cup of the flour in a medium-sized bowl and add the yeast mixture. Stir together until the milk is absorbed by the flour. Transfer this sponge to your work surface and wash and dry the bowl. Return the sponge to the bowl and cover it with the remaining 4 cups flour. Let the sponge rise for 1 hour.

3. With a wooden spoon, beat the remaining $\frac{1}{2}$ cup of sugar, salt, and the 6 eggs into the sponge and dry flour. Beat in the $\frac{3}{4}$-pound butter, 3 to 4 tablespoons at a time, until it is triple in volume. This will take about 3 hours.

4. With a wooden spoon, stir the dough down, cover with plastic wrap, and refrigerate for 2 hours. Stir the dough down, cover it again, and chill it overnight.

5. On a lightly floured surface, roll out one-fourth of the brioche dough to a thickness of $\frac{1}{4}$ inch. Line the bottom and sides of a lightly buttered 9-inch layer cake pan with the brioche dough and trim off the excess along the top edge of the pan.

6. Roll out the remaining dough into a 14-by-27-inch rectangle and brush it with the beaten egg white. Combine $\frac{1}{2}$ cup of the nuts, currants, sugar, and cinnamon, and sprinkle the mixture over the dough. Cover with a piece of wax paper and with a rolling pin press the filling into the dough. Remove the wax paper and roll the dough lengthwise into a cylinder. Cut the cylinder into 9 equal rounds.

7. Place the rolls cut side up, on the bottom of the brioche-lined cake tin, spacing them as evenly as possible. Brush the tops and all the exposed dough with the beaten egg and let the cake rise to triple in volume. This will take about 3 hours.

8. Preheat the oven to 350°.

9. Again brush the cake with beaten egg, and then bake it on a rack in the middle of the oven for 40 minutes, or until it turns a deep golden brown. Let the cake cool in the pan for 20 minutes before transferring it to a cake rack to cool completely.

Puff Pastry

Although puff pastry is not that difficult to make, my students and most people in general are often intimidated by the lengthy instructions it requires. Actually, there are only four basic ingredients to work with and as soon as you proceed through the recipe you will find that the steps are simple and repetitive and you will be delighted with your success in making this versatile pastry. Wrapped in aluminum foil, puff pastry can be refrigerated for up to two days before it is used, or it can be frozen for months. Defrost the pastry in the refrigerator before shaping it.

YIELD: 3 POUNDS

4½ cups all-purpose flour
1¼ pounds unsalted butter
  (5 sticks)
1 cup ice water
½ teaspoon salt

1. Place ½ cup of the flour in a medium-sized bowl. Cut 4 sticks of the butter into ½-inch cubes, adding the cubes to the flour as you cut. With your hands, thoroughly combine the butter and flour until they are well blended. Shape this butter-flour mixture into a 4-by-4-inch square, cover it with plastic wrap and place it in the refrigerator to chill.

2. Place the remaining 4 cups of flour in the same bowl, and cut the remaining 1 stick of butter into cubes, adding it to the flour in the same fashion as in Step 1. Add the ice water and salt, and stir with a wooden spoon until the water is absorbed by the flour. Transfer the dough to your work surface and knead it thoroughly for about 5 minutes until it becomes a smooth mass. Shape the dough into a ball, cover it with plastic wrap, and place it in the refrigerator to rest and chill for 15 minutes.

3. Remove the ball of dough from the refrigerator and place it on a lightly floured work surface. Using a sharp knife, cut a 1-inch-deep crisscross into the top of the dough. Push out each corner of the dough to resemble a four leaf clover and, with a lightly floured rolling pin, elongate these corners, creating an ''X'' that measures 17 inches across. (See the accompanying illustration.)

4. Remove the butter-flour square from the refrigerator and

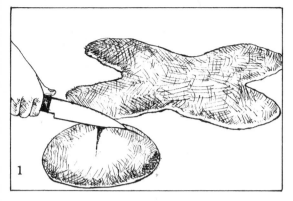

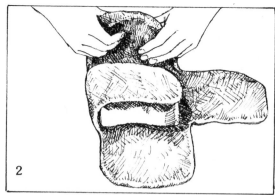

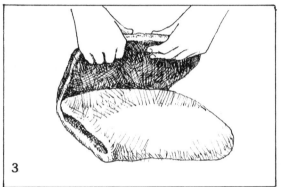

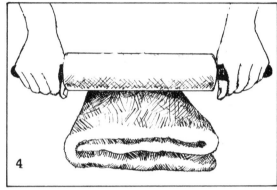

Rolling puff pastry. 1. *Using a knife, make a cross-cut in the dough and roll out each corner until you have an X that measures 17 inches across.* 2. *Center the butter–flour square at the center of the dough and, one at a time, fold each corner of dough over it, making a neat package.* 3. *Roll the dough into a rectangle* *that measures about 10 inches by 20 inches (use a ruler to check it). Fold the dough crosswise in thirds after the first and all subsequent rollings.* 4. *Start each rolling with an open end of the dough facing you and roll lengthwise, working out from the center.*

place it on the center of the X. One at a time, fold each corner of the dough up over the butter, making a neat package and completely encasing the butter in the dough. With the flat of your hands, press the package into a 7-inch square, then wrap it in plastic wrap and refrigerate for 30 minutes to let the dough rest and chill.

5. Remove the package of dough from the refrigerator and roll it out on a lightly floured surface into a rectangle that measures 12 inches wide and 21 inches long. Check the measurements with a ruler. Always roll with even pressure from the center of the dough outward. Do not roll over the edge of the dough. If butter shows through the dough on

any rolling, cover it with flour. With a dry pastry brush dust off any excess flour remaining on the surface of the dough. Neatly fold the dough crosswise into thirds, cover it with plastic wrap, and refrigerate for 30 minutes.

6. Remove the dough from the refrigerator and place it on a lightly floured work surface with one of the narrow, open ends facing you. Roll the dough out, just as you did the first time, but this time make a rectangle that measures 14 by 24 inches. Dust the excess flour from the pastry, and again fold it crosswise into three layers. Return the pastry to the refrigerator to chill and rest for 30 minutes.

7. Repeat the last step four more times, allowing the dough to chill and rest 30 minutes between each rolling. To help you remember, keep track of the number of the rolling on a slip of paper, or mark the appropriate number with light finger impressions on top of the dough. After the last fold, wrap the dough again. Place it in the refrigerator to rest and chill for at least 2 hours, or preferably overnight, before shaping it.

Poppy Seed Wreath

YIELD: 8 TO 10 SERVINGS

1 tablespoon unsalted butter, softened, plus 4 tablespoons unsalted butter
1 package active dry yeast
¼ cup granulated sugar
1 cup milk, brought to a boil and cooled to lukewarm (110° to 115°)
5 to 6 cups all-purpose flour
2 teaspoons salt
3 large eggs
1 egg, beaten
½ cup of poppy seeds

1. Grease a large cookie sheet with the tablespoon of softened butter. Remove the bottom from an empty coffee can and wash and dry the can thoroughly. Butter the outside of the can and place it upright at the center of the cookie sheet. Set the cookie sheet aside.

2. Stir the yeast and ½ teaspoon of the sugar into the warm milk. Let the mixture stand until it foams, about 4 to 6 minutes.

3. In a large bowl, combine the remaining sugar, 5 cups of flour, the salt, 3 eggs, and the remaining butter. Add the yeast mixture. Stir all the ingredients together until the milk is absorbed by the flour. Remove the dough from the bowl and place it on a lightly floured work surface.

4. Knead the dough by pushing it forward and folding it back in half on top of itself. Continue to knead the dough

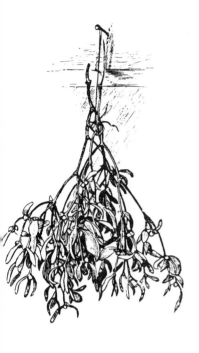

for 15 to 20 minutes, or until it is smooth and elastic. When necessary, sprinkle the dough with enough flour to keep it from sticking to your hands or the surface.

5. Place the dough in a large buttered bowl and turn it to coat it with butter. Cover the dough with plastic wrap or a towel and let it rise for about 1 hour, or until it doubles in size.

6. Punch the dough down in the bowl, coat it with butter as before, cover, and let it rise for the second time until double in size.

7. Transfer the risen dough from the bowl to the work surface and press it flat with the palms of your hands. Divide the dough into 3 equal pieces, and let them rest for 5 minutes.

8. With the palms of your hands and working the dough from the center outwards, roll each piece of dough into a 16- to 18-inch-long cylinder. Overlap the 3 cylinders of dough at one end and weight them down with a small, heavy saucepan so that you can braid them. Separate the cylinders by fanning them out slightly. Now start to braid them by lifting the middle piece and crossing the 2 outer pieces under it. Then set the middle piece down and cross the outer ones *over* it. Continue braiding in this fashion until you reach the ends.

9. Wrap the braid around the base of the coffee can, overlapping and pressing the ends together securely. Brush the wreath with the beaten egg and let it rise for 1 hour, or until doubled in size.

10. Preheat oven to 375°.

11. Brush the braid again with the beaten egg and sprinkle it with the poppy seeds. Bake on a rack in the middle of the oven for 40 to 45 minutes, or until deep brown. Remove the coffee can and transfer the wreath to a wire rack to cool.

Mincemeat Tartlets

The dryness of the hard-cooked egg yolks in this recipe helps to keep the pastry from absorbing the moisture in the mincemeat. Therefore, the tartlets can be made one day in advance. Store them in a cool place, but do not refrigerate.

YIELD: 8 TO 10 FOUR-INCH TARTLETS

2 cups all-purpose flour
$\frac{1}{4}$ teaspoon salt
$\frac{1}{4}$ cup granulated sugar
12 tablespoons unsalted butter (1$\frac{1}{2}$ sticks)
2 large egg yolks
2 hard-cooked egg yolks, sieved
2 teaspoons grated lemon rind
4 cups mincemeat (page 7)
4 cups cored, peeled, and finely chopped apples or pears

1. Place all the ingredients, except for the mincemeat and apples or pears in a large bowl. With your hands, work the ingredients together until they form a well-blended pastry with no streaks of egg yolk showing. Wrap the pastry in plastic wrap and refrigerate for at least 1 hour.

2. Mix the mincemeat and apples or pears together.

3. Preheat the oven to 375°.

4. Remove the pastry from the refrigerator and cut off enough to make one tart. Roll the pastry between 2 pieces of wax paper to a thickness of a little more than $\frac{1}{8}$ inch. Peel off the top piece of the wax paper; then pick up the bottom piece and invert the pastry over a 4-inch tartlet pan. Peel off and discard the paper. Gently press the pastry against the bottom and sides of the pan; then press any excess against the top edge of the pan to remove it. The first tart will be your guide as to how much pastry is needed to line each pan. If you were short on the first one, simply patch it with additional pastry. If you had too much pastry, return it to the refrigerator to chill and use it later for the lattice top. Continue to line the pans. Gather all the scraps of pastry together and chill.

5. Fill each tartlet pan with some of the mincemeat mixture.

6. To make a lattice top for the tartlets, roll out the remaining pastry between sheets of wax paper to make a rectangle about $\frac{1}{4}$ inch thick. Using a pastry wheel or knife, cut $\frac{1}{4}$-inch-wide strips of pastry that are slightly longer than the diameter of the tartlet pan. Spacing them evenly, lay 3 strips of pastry across the top of the tartlet. Cross them with 3 more strips placed at right angles on top of them. Trim off the ends of the strips by pressing them against the outside edge of the tartlet pan.

7. Place the mincemeat tartlets on a large cookie sheet and

bake on a rack in the middle of the oven for about 40 minutes or until the pastry is nicely browned. Transfer the tartlets to wire racks and let them cool in their pans.

Christmas Log with Mocha Butter Cream

If you have the freezer space, this whimsical French Christmas cake, known in France as a *bûche de Noël,* can be made weeks before the holidays to give as a gift. After completing the cake decoration place the cake in the freezer until the butter cream is hard; then cover it with several layers of plastic wrap and return it to the freezer for storage. The perfect solution for transporting the cake is a florist's flower box. Be sure to tell the lucky recipient to unwrap the Christmas log while it is very cold to avoid damaging the butter-cream bark, but to let the cake come to room temperature before serving.

Cake

YIELD: 6 TO 8 SERVINGS

6 large eggs, at room
    temperature
1 cup granulated sugar
$\frac{1}{2}$ teaspoon vanilla extract
1 cup all-purpose flour
6 tablespoons butter,
    melted and cooled to
    room temperature

1. Preheat the oven to 350°.

2. Grease the inside of a $17\frac{1}{2}$-by-11-inch jelly-roll pan with 1 tablespoon of the melted butter. Line the pan with wax paper, and coat the paper with an additional tablespoon of the butter. Sprinkle the paper with flour, shake the pan to coat the paper with the flour, then rap the pan to remove any excess.

3. Using an electric mixer, beat the eggs, sugar, and vanilla extract together until the mixture triples in volume and runs off the beater in thick ribbons.

4. Add $\frac{1}{2}$ cup of the flour at a time, sprinkling it over the egg mixture and then folding it in with a large rubber spatula. Watch carefully for any pockets of dry flour and fold them in. Fold in the remaining cooled butter, 2 tablespoons at a time.

5. Pour and scrape the batter into the prepared pan and bake on a rack in the middle of the oven for 15 to 20 minutes, or until the cake is a light golden brown and shrinks slightly from the sides of the pan.

6. Keeping the cake on the wax paper, lift it from the pan and let it cool for 15 minutes on a wire rack. Remove the

cake from the rack and roll it and the wax paper up length-wise. Set the cake aside while making the butter cream.

Butter Cream

4 large egg whites
1 cup granulated sugar
1 teaspoon vanilla extract
1½ cups confectioners'
  sugar
¾ pound unsalted butter (3
  sticks), softened
2 teaspoons unsweetened
  cocoa
Green food coloring
2 tablespoons instant
  espresso

1. Combine the egg whites, granulated sugar, and vanilla in the bowl of an electric mixer. Place the bowl in a bath of barely simmering water and beat with a wire whisk until the sugar completely dissolves.

2. Remove the egg-white mixture from the water bath. Beat with the electric mixer on high speed until the mixture returns to room temperature and is very thick. Reduce the speed to medium, and gradually add the confectioners' sugar. Beat in the softened butter 4 tablespoons at a time. Return the mixer to high speed and continue to beat the butter cream until it is light and fluffy.

3. Place ¼ cup of the butter cream in a very small bowl, beat in the unsweetened cocoa, and set aside.

4. Place 2 tablespoons of the butter cream in a second small bowl. Squeeze a drop of green food coloring onto a saucer and, using a toothpick, transfer a tiny bit of the coloring to the butter cream. With a small spoon, blend them together. Gradually add more color in the same fashion until you have a shade you like for pastel green leaves. Set aside.

5. With a whisk or electric beater, beat the espresso into the remaining butter cream. Set aside.

Meringue Mushrooms

2 large egg whites
Pinch salt
¼ cup granulated sugar
¼ teaspoon vanilla extract

1. Preheat the oven to 200°

2. Lightly butter and flour a large cookie sheet.

3. In a medium-size bowl, beat the egg whites until they form soft peaks when the beater is lifted. Add the salt, gradually add the sugar, and then the vanilla. Continue to beat the egg whites until they hold firm peaks.

4. Put the meringue in a pastry bag fitted with a number 3 (¼ inch) plain tip. Force the meringue through the pastry bag onto the baking sheet to form 1-inch-wide domes for the

mushroom caps, then make cones to serve as the stems (see the accompanying illustration).

5. Bake on a rack in the middle of the oven for 45 minutes to 1 hour, or until the meringue is dry and the pieces can be easily pulled off the baking sheet. Transfer the caps and stems to a wire rack to cool.

6. To assemble the mushrooms, make a hole in the bottom of each cap with the tip of a paring knife. Dip the pointed end of each cone into a little butter cream and gently insert the end into the hole in the cap. Place three of the mushrooms on top of the Christmas log and arrange the remaining mushrooms around the cake.

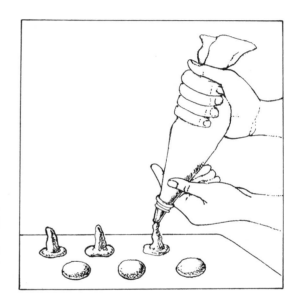

Shaping meringue mushrooms. *To make the mushroom caps, force meringue through a pastry bag fitted with a number 3 plain tip to form 1-inch-wide domes. To make the stems, lift the pastry bag as you are forcing the meringue through it to make 1½-inch-high-cones.*

Assembling the Cake

1. Unroll the cooled cake and, with a metal icing spatula, spread a thin layer of the coffee butter cream over the top. Using the wax paper as an aid, but removing it as you go, roll the cake up lengthwise and, with both hands transfer the roll to a cookie sheet or inverted jelly-roll pan. Slice a piece of cake from each end of the roll at the same diagonal so the thickest side of each piece is no more than 1 inch wide. Reserve one of the pieces.

2. With a metal spatula, spread most of the coffee butter cream thickly over all but the ends of the roll. Place the reserved slice of cake on top of the roll but slightly off center to resemble the stump of a large branch. Cover the sides of the branch stump with coffee butter cream, leaving the cut top end bare.

3. To simulate tree bark, draw rough and slightly wavy lines with the tines of a dinner fork along the length of the roll, starting at the bottom of one side and at one end of the roll. Repeat, making similar parallel lines the length of the cake and moving a fork width farther each time, until the entire cake has a barklike texture. Cover both ends of the log and the cut end of the branch stump with the cocoa butter cream.

4. Spoon the green butter cream into a paper decorating cone (see the directions for making one below) and, with a scissors, cut a tiny portion off the tip of the cone. Make four or five curving green lines the length of the log to simulate ivy vines.

5. Using the scissors again, clip a V-shaped notch at the end of the paper cone by making a shallow $\frac{1}{4}$-inch-deep cut from each side to the center of the cone. Now pipe small butter-cream leaves along the vines, making an entire leaf with each stroke of the cone.

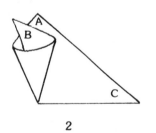

1

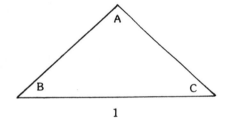

2

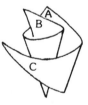

3

4

Making a paper pastry cone. *Cut a triangle of parchment paper that is 21 inches long on one side and 15 inches long on the other two sides, or use a piece of precut paper, the same size, which is available in most cookware shops.* 1. *Place the triangle so that the longest edge is at the bottom.* 2. *Fold one of the side corners, in this case B, in and under toward A, making a cone whose tip is directly below A.* 3. *Fold the opposite corner of the triangle (C) tightly around the cone.* 4. *Using scissors, cut the tip off the cone as instructed in the recipe: about $\frac{1}{8}$ inch to draw a fine line, more to make wider lines or designs.*

Walnut Cake

Cake

YIELD: 10 TO 12 SERVINGS

6 large eggs, at room
  temperature
1 cup granulated sugar
1½ teaspoons vanilla extract
1½ cups all-purpose flour,
  sifted
6 tablespoons unsalted
  butter, melted and
  cooled to room
  temperature

1. Preheat the oven to 350°.

2. Lightly butter the inside of a 9-inch cake pan, and sprinkle it with flour. Invert the pan and tap it to remove any excess flour.

3. Using an electric mixer, beat the eggs, sugar, and vanilla extract together until the mixture triples in volume and runs off the beater in thick ribbons.

4. Add ½ cup of the flour at a time, sprinkling it over the egg mixture and then folding it in with a large rubber spatula. Watch carefully for any pockets of dry flour and fold them in. Fold in the melted butter 2 tablespoons at a time.

5. Scrape the batter into the prepared pan and bake on a rack in the middle of the oven for 20 to 25 minutes, or until the cake is a light golden brown and shrinks slightly from the sides of the pan. Remove the cake from the oven and let it cool in the pan on a wire rack.

Butter Cream

4 large egg whites
1 cup granulated sugar
1 teaspoon vanilla extract
1½ cups confectioners'
  sugar
¾ pound (3 sticks) butter,
  softened
3 tablespoons dark rum
1 cup ground walnuts
Green food color, optional
1½ cups almonds, toasted
  and coarsely chopped

1. Combine the egg whites, granulated sugar, and vanilla extract in the bowl of an electric mixer. Place the bowl in a bath of barely simmering water, and beat with a wire whisk until the sugar completely dissolves.

2. Remove the egg white mixture from the water bath, and beat with the electric mixer on high speed until it returns to room temperature and is very thick. Reduce the speed to medium and gradually add the confectioners' sugar. Beat in the softened butter 4 tablespoons at a time, then add the rum and ground walnuts.

3. Squeeze a few drops of green food color onto a saucer and, using a toothpick, transfer a tiny bit of the coloring to the butter cream and blend them together. Gradually add more color in the same fashion until the butter cream is a pastel green.

4. When the cake has cooled, remove it from the pan, cut it horizontally into 2 layers, and, with a metal spatula, spread 4 tablespoons of the butter cream evenly on top of the bottom layer. Set the second layer on top, and spread the remaining butter cream evenly over the entire cake.

5. Place the toasted almonds on a large plate. Hold the frosted cake over the plate with one hand and, using the other hand, scoop up the toasted almonds and press them against the sides of the cake.

Decoration

8 tablespoons marzipan (page 58)
$\frac{1}{4}$ *teaspoon unsweetened cocoa*
7 walnut halves
Liquid green food coloring

1. To make marzipan walnut shell halves, work the cocoa into 7 teaspoons of the marzipan and, 1 teaspoon at a time, press this marzipan into a lightly oiled walnut mold so that it lines the sides. (Walnut molds are available in specialty food-equipment shops.) Fill the center of the mold with 1 teaspoon of the plain marzipan. Press a walnut half into the marzipan walnut shell and release the decoration from the mold with the tip of a paring knife.

Making a marzipan walnut. *To shape the shell of the nut, line a metal walnut mold with cocoa-colored marzipan. Then make a small ball of natural-colored marzipan and press it into the shell (1). Finally, press a walnut half into the center of the marzipan shell (2).*

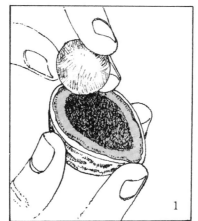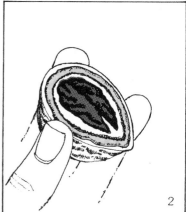

2. To make decorative marzipan leaves, tint the remaining marzipan with a little green food coloring. Roll this marzipan between two pieces of waxed paper until it is $\frac{1}{8}$-inch thick. Cut the leaves out with a paring knife. See the first color section for a picture of the decorated cake.

Panettone

YIELD: 6 TO 8 SERVINGS

1 package active dry yeast
Pinch, plus ⅓ cup
*   granulated sugar*
¼ cup lukewarm water
*   (110° to 115°)*
2¾ to 3 cups all-purpose
*   flour*
½ cup milk
6 large egg yolks
½ teaspoon salt
8 tablespoons unsalted
*   butter (1 stick), softened*
1½ teaspoons grated lemon
*   rind*
1 teaspoon vanilla extract
¼ cup diced citron
¼ cup sultana raisins
¼ cup dark raisins
2 tablespoons unsalted
*   butter, melted*

1. Line a 1-pound coffee can with a double thickness of wax paper.

2. Stir the yeast together with the pinch of sugar into the warm water. Let the mixture stand until it foams, about 4 to 6 minutes.

3. In a large bowl, combine the remaining ⅓ cup of sugar, 2¾ cups of the flour, the milk, egg yolks, salt, butter, grated lemon rind, and vanilla. Stir all the ingredients together until the liquids are absorbed by the flour. Remove the dough from the bowl and place it on a lightly floured surface.

4. Knead the dough by pushing it forward and folding it back in half on top of itself. Continue to knead the dough for 15 to 20 minutes, or until it is smooth and elastic. Sprinkle the dough, when necessary, with enough flour to keep it from sticking to your hands or the work surface.

5. Place the dough in a large buttered bowl and turn it to coat it with butter. Cover the dough with plastic wrap or a towel, and let it rise for about 1 hour, or until it doubles in size.

6. Transfer the risen dough from the bowl to the work surface, and very gently knead the citron and light and dark raisins into it only until the fruit is well incorporated. Kneading too much will discolor the dough.

7. Return the dough to a clean well-buttered bowl, and again turn it to coat it with butter. Cover the bowl and let the dough rise for 1 hour, or until it doubles in size.

8. Turn the dough out onto the work surface, and press it flat with the palms of your hands. Shape it into a ball and press the ball into the lined coffee can. Brush the top of the dough with the melted butter, cover the can, and let the dough rise for 45 minutes, or until it doubles in size.

9. Preheat the oven to 400°.

10. Bake the panettone on a rack in the middle of the oven (if the coffee can is too high, lower the rack one notch) for

15 minutes, then lower the heat to 375° and continue to bake for an additional 15 to 20 minutes, or until the top of the cake is golden brown.

11. Let the panettone cool in the coffee can for 10 minutes before removing the can and transferring the cake to a wire rack to cool completely.

Pithiviers

This cake is named for the French town of Pithiviers, which is noted for its almond pastries.

YIELD: 8 SERVINGS

1¼ cups blanched almonds,
 toasted and ground
¼ cup granulated sugar
4 tablespoons unsalted
 butter
2 large egg yolks
½ teaspoon vanilla extract
1 teaspoon freshly grated
 lemon rind
2 tablespoons dark rum
1 pound puff pastry
 (pages 30–32)
1 egg, beaten
½ cup confectioners' sugar

1. In a large bowl, mix the ground almonds, granulated sugar, butter, egg yolks, vanilla, lemon rind and dark rum until they are well blended. With your hands, shape the mixture into a 6-inch flat cake, wrap it in plastic wrap, and refrigerate for at least 30 minutes.

2. Run cold water over a large cookie sheet, shake off the excess, and set it aside.

3. Cut the pastry in half and return one of the halves to the refrigerator. On a lightly floured surface, roll the pastry to a thickness of about ¼ inch and transfer it to the cookie sheet.

4. Invert an 8-inch diameter dinner plate over the pastry and, using a sharp knife and the rim of the plate as a guide, cut out a disk of pastry. Remove the second piece of pastry from the refrigerator and roll it out as described but do not cut it into a disk.

5. Center the almond cake on the 8-inch pastry disk and, with a pastry brush and water, dampen the exposed pastry around it. Gently lift the second piece of pastry and set it on top of the almond cake filling so it covers the bottom pastry as well. With your fingertips, press the top and bottom layers of pastry together. Invert a 9-inch layer-cake pan, center it on the pithiviers and, with a sharp knife and using the edge of the pan as a guide, trim off the excess pastry. With the back of a paring knife, make ¼-inch-deep

indentations about 1 inch apart all around the edge of the pastry. Brush the pithiviers with the beaten egg and place it in the refrigerator to rest and chill for at least 30 minutes. Reserve the beaten egg.

6. With the wide end of a number 5 star tube, cut a vent in the top center of the pastry. Brush the pastry again with the egg yolk.

7. Preheat the oven to 425°.

8. To decorate the pithiviers, use the back of a paring knife to make $\frac{1}{4}$-inch-long marks at $\frac{1}{2}$-inch intervals around the outer edge of the pastry. In a similar fashion, press a curving line from the vent to the closest mark on the outer edge of the pastry. Repeat, moving around the cake, to create a fluted design. (See the illustration below.) Set the baking sheet on a rack in the middle of the oven and bake the cake for 10 minutes. Reduce the heat to 375° and continue to bake the pithiviers for an additional 20 minutes, or until it turns a deep golden color.

9. Remove the cake from the oven and sieve the confectioners' sugar over the top. Return the cake to the oven. Increase the heat to 500° and bake the cake for 5 minutes, or until the sugar caramelizes. Transfer the cake from the baking sheet to a wire rack to cool.

Decorating a pithiviers cake. With the back of a paring knife, make $\frac{1}{4}$-inch-long indentations at $\frac{1}{2}$-inch intervals around the bottom edge of the cake. Then, using the back of the knife, draw a sweeping curved line from the vent at the top of the cake to each of the marks along the bottom.

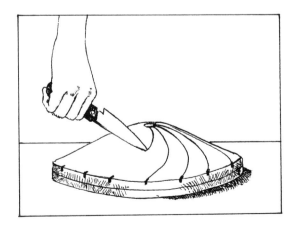

Stollen

Stollen can be made and frozen as soon as fresh candied fruit is available in the fall, usually in late September. Whenever you bake stollen, always remember that they should age in the refrigerator, or in any cool place, for two weeks before serving or freezing to let the flavors marry. If you wish to make smaller loaves as gifts, divide this recipe into four portions, following the same instructions, and reduce the baking time to 20 to 30 minutes. Stollen is delicious for breakfast, afternoon tea, or for a bedtime snack. I love it any time, topped with sweet butter, and some people like to warm it or even toast it before serving.

YIELD: TWO 8-BY-3-INCH-
LONG LOAVES

$\frac{1}{2}$ cup seedless raisins
$\frac{1}{2}$ cup dried currants
1 cup mixed candied citrus
   peel
$\frac{1}{2}$ cup candied cherries
$\frac{1}{2}$ cup dark rum or brandy
2 packages active dry yeast
$\frac{1}{2}$ teaspoon, plus $\frac{3}{4}$ cup,
   granulated sugar
$1\frac{1}{2}$ cups milk, brought to a
   boil and allowed to cool
   to lukewarm (110° to
   115°)
6 cups all-purpose flour
$\frac{1}{2}$ teaspoon salt
$\frac{1}{4}$ teaspoon ground
   cardamom
3 large eggs
1 teaspoon grated lemon
   rind
$\frac{3}{4}$ teaspoon almond extract
12 tablespoons unsalted
   butter ($1\frac{1}{2}$ sticks),
   softened
1 cup blanched almonds,
   coarsely chopped
$\frac{1}{4}$ cup melted butter
$\frac{1}{2}$ cup confectioners' sugar

1. Soak the raisins, currants, candied citrus peel and cherries in the rum or brandy overnight, or for several days, stirring them occasionally.

2. Stir the yeast and $\frac{1}{2}$ teaspoon of the sugar into the warm milk. Let the mixture stand until it foams, about 4 to 6 minutes.

3. In a large bowl, combine the $\frac{3}{4}$ cup sugar, the flour, salt, cardamom, eggs, grated lemon rind, almond extract, softened butter, and the yeast-milk mixture. Stir all the ingredients together until the milk is absorbed by the flour. Remove the dough from the bowl and place it on a lightly floured surface.

4. Knead the dough by pushing it forward and folding it back in half on top of itself. Continue to knead the dough for 15 to 20 minutes, or until it is smooth and elastic. When necessary, sprinkle the dough with enough flour to keep it from sticking to your hands or the work surface.

5. Place the dough in a large buttered bowl and turn it to coat it with butter. Cover the dough with plastic wrap or a towel, and let it rise for about 1 hour, or until it doubles in size.

6. Pour off any excess brandy or rum from the fruit and pat the fruit dry with paper toweling. Return the fruit to a bowl and stir in the chopped almonds.

7. Transfer the risen dough from the bowl to the work surface, and very gently knead the fruit and nuts into it. Knead only until the fruit and nuts are well incorporated. Kneading too much will discolor the dough.

8. Return the dough to a clean, well-buttered bowl, and again turn it to coat it with butter. Cover the bowl and let the dough rise for $1\frac{1}{2}$ to 2 hours, or until it doubles in size.

9. Turn the dough out on the work surface, and press it flat with the palms of your hands. Divide the dough into two equal pieces. Roll one half of the dough into a rough 10-by-16-inch rectangle. Brush it with the melted butter, then fold one long side to the center. Brush the top of that side with a little additional butter. Fold the opposite side over to cover two thirds of the first side. Slightly taper both ends of the loaf.

10. Place the shaped loaf on a lightly buttered cookie sheet. Repeat the same procedure for the other half of the dough. Let the stollen rise again 1 to $1\frac{1}{2}$ hours, or until the loaves double in size.

11. Preheat the oven to 375°.

12. Bake the stollen on a rack in the middle of the oven for 35 to 45 minutes, or until they turn a deep golden brown. Transfer the stollen to wire racks to cool. Before serving, dust them with sifted confectioners' sugar.

White Bread

YIELD: ONE 9-BY-5-BY-3-INCH LOAF

1 package active dry yeast
½ teaspoon granulated sugar
¾ cup lukewarm water (110° to 115°)
4½ to 5 cups all-purpose flour
2½ teaspoons salt
6 tablespoons unsalted butter, softened
1¼ cups milk
1 whole egg, beaten

1. Lightly butter a 9-by-5-by 3-inch loaf pan.

2. Stir the yeast and sugar into the warm water. Let the mixture stand until it foams, about 4 to 6 minutes.

3. In a large bowl, combine the flour, salt, butter, milk, and yeast mixture. Stir all the ingredients together until the liquids are absorbed by the flour. Remove the dough from the bowl and place it on a lightly floured work surface.

4. Knead the dough by pushing it forward and folding it back in half on top of itself. Continue to knead the dough for 15 to 20 minutes, or until it is smooth and elastic. When necessary, sprinkle the dough with enough flour to keep it from sticking to your hands or the work surface.

5. Place the dough in a large buttered bowl and turn it to coat it with butter. Cover the dough with plastic wrap or a towel and let it rise for about 1 hour, or until it doubles in size.

6. Punch the dough down in the bowl, coat it as before with butter, cover, and let it rise for the second time until double in size.

7. Transfer the dough from the bowl to the work surface and press it flat with the palms of your hands. Roll the dough into a cylinder and place it in the prepared loaf pan, tucking the ends under. With your fingers, push the dough into the corners and sides of the pan, shaping the loaf so it is slightly higher in the center.

8. Brush the top of the loaf with the beaten egg, cover with a towel, and let the dough rise until the center of the loaf reaches the top of the pan.

9. Preheat the oven to 375°.

10. Brush the top of the loaf with the egg again, and bake the loaf on a rack in the middle of the oven for 40 to 45 minutes, or until it is a rich brown color. Remove the loaf from the pan and set it on a wire rack to cool.

Whole Wheat Bread

YIELD: ONE 12-BY-5-INCH LOAF

2 packages active dry yeast
½ teaspoon granulated sugar
½ cup lukewarm water (110° to 115°)
3 cups stone-ground whole wheat flour
3 to 4 cups all-purpose flour
4 teaspoons salt
2½ cups milk, brought to a boil and allowed to cool to lukewarm (110° to 115°)
½ cup honey
1 whole egg, beaten

1. Butter a 12-by-5-by-3-inch loaf pan and set it aside.

2. Stir the yeast and the sugar into the lukewarm water. Let the mixture stand until it foams, about 4 to 6 minutes.

3. In a large bowl, combine the whole wheat flour, 3 cups of the all-purpose flour, the salt, milk, honey, and the yeast mixture. Stir all the ingredients together until the liquid is absorbed by the flour. Remove the dough from the bowl and place it on a lightly floured surface.

4. Knead the dough by pushing it forward and folding it back in half on top of itself. Continue to knead the dough for 15 to 20 minutes, or until it is smooth and elastic. When necessary, sprinkle the dough with enough flour to keep it from sticking to your hands or the work surface.

5. Place the dough in a large buttered bowl and turn it to coat it with butter. Cover the dough with plastic wrap or a towel and let it rise for about 1½ hours, or until it doubles in size.

6. Punch the dough down in the bowl, coat it with butter as before, cover, and let it rise for the second time until it doubles in·size.

7. Transfer the dough from the bowl to the work surface and press it flat with the palms of your hands. Roll the dough into a cylinder and place it in the prepared loaf pan, tucking the ends under. With your fingers, push the dough into the corners and sides of the pan, shaping the loaf so it is slightly higher in the center.

8. Brush the top of the loaf with the beaten egg, cover with a towel, and let the dough rise until the center of the loaf reaches the top of the pan.

9. Preheat the oven to 375°.

10. Brush the top of the loaf again, and bake the bread on a rack in the middle of the oven for 40 to 45 minutes or until it is a rich brown. Remove the loaf from the pan and set it on a wire rack to cool.

Star of Zurich

Scarcely known in this country, this Swiss holiday cake is an unusual combination of puff pastry and meringue. Baking the cake briefly in a very hot oven produces both a light and flaky puff pastry and a wonderfully chewy meringue.

YIELD: 6 TO 8 SERVINGS

1 pound puff pastry (pages 30–32), or puff pastry scraps, chilled
1 egg, lightly beaten
3 large egg whites, at room temperature
$\frac{1}{3}$ cup granulated sugar
$\frac{1}{2}$ cup almonds, toasted and ground
$\frac{1}{2}$ cup unsweetened coconut, grated
3 tablespoons confectioners' sugar
$1\frac{1}{2}$ cups heavy cream, chilled
$\frac{1}{2}$ teaspoon vanilla extract
Candied cherries or violets and angelica for decorating

1. Using parchment paper or cardboard, cut out a star-shaped template, or pattern, as illustrated.

2. Roll out the puff pastry to a thickness of $\frac{1}{4}$ inch, then transfer it to a large dampened cookie sheet. Using a sharp knife and the template as a guide, cut a star out of the puff pastry. With a fork, prick the entire surface of the puff pastry. Using a pastry brush, coat about $\frac{1}{2}$ inch along the outer edge of the pastry star with the beaten egg.

3. From the remaining pastry, cut out $\frac{1}{2}$-inch-wide strips and apply them to the edge of the star, pressing down gently so they will stick to the egg and the bottom pastry and cutting the ends neatly to conform to the points of the star. Brush the top of each strip with beaten egg and refrigerate the pastry to chill and rest for at least 2 hours.

4. Preheat the oven to 425°.

5. Beat the egg whites to soft peaks, then gradually add the granulated sugar and continue to beat until the whites form a stiff meringue. With a rubber spatula, fold in the almonds and coconut. Fill the star with meringue, spreading it to the inside edge of the outer strips and mounding it slightly in the center.

6. Bake the star on a rack in the middle of the oven for 20 minutes, reduce the heat to 375°, and continue to bake an additional 10 minutes, or until the pastry is a golden brown. Transfer the star to a wire rack to cool.

7. Just before serving, sift 1 tablespoon of confectioners' sugar over the meringue portion of the star. Next, whip the cream with the remaining 2 tablespoons of confectioners' sugar and the vanilla extract until it holds firm but not stiff peaks. Using a pastry bag fitted with a number 5 star tube, pipe the whipped cream around the top edge of the star. Decorate the cream with the candied cherries or violets and angelica. (See the first color section.)

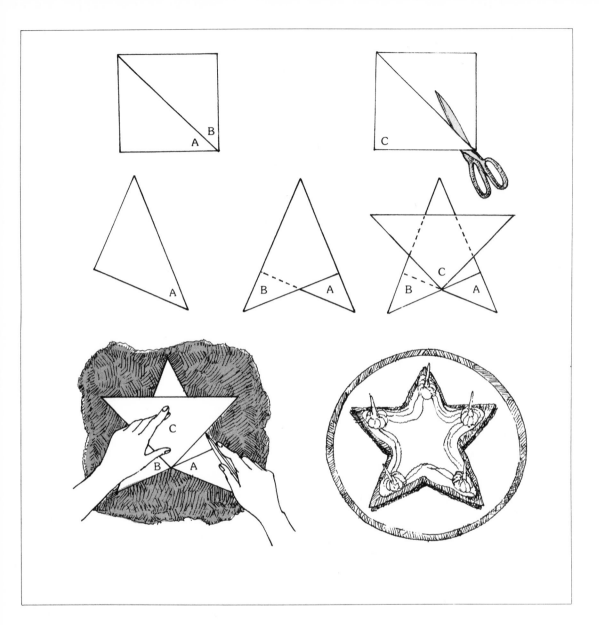

Making a star template and cutting a star of Zurich.

Cut two 12-inch squares from baker's parchment or any stiff, clean paper. Cut each square in half diagonally, forming two equal triangles. Discard one triangle; then label the remaining three triangles a, b, and c and arrange them to make a star as shown. Tape the pieces together and lay the star template on rolled-out pastry that has been set on a baking sheet. Cut around the template with a thin, sharp knife.

King's Cake

By an ancient tradition in both France and England, the person that gets the favor (in this case a the pecan half) hidden in this special Twelfth Night cake has good luck for the rest of the year. The colored sugar is a New Orleans' touch.

Cake

YIELD: 6 TO 8 SERVINGS

1 package active dry yeast
½ cup granulated sugar
¼ cup lukewarm water
   (110° to 115°)
4 to 4½ cups all-purpose
   flour
2 teaspoons salt
½ teaspoon freshly ground
   nutmeg
2 teaspoons finely grated
   lemon peel
¾ cup milk
5 large egg yolks
8 tablespoons unsalted
   butter (1 stick), softened
⅔ cup finely chopped citron
1 pecan half
1 egg yolk, beaten

1. Stir the yeast and ½ teaspoon of the sugar into the lukewarm water. Let the mixture stand until it foams, about 4 to 6 minutes.

2. In a large bowl, combine the remaining sugar, 4 cups of the flour, the salt, nutmeg, lemon peel, milk, egg yolks, butter, and the yeast mixture. Stir all the ingredients together until the liquid is absorbed by the flour. Remove the dough from the bowl and place it on a lightly floured work surface.

3. Knead the dough by pushing it forward and folding it back in half on top of itself. Continue to knead the dough for 15 to 20 minutes, or until it is smooth and elastic. When necessary, sprinkle the dough with enough flour to keep it from sticking to your hands or the work surface.

4. Place the dough in a large buttered bowl and turn it to coat it with butter. Cover the bowl with plastic wrap or a towel, and let the dough rise for about 1 hour, or until it doubles in size.

5. Transfer the dough from the bowl to the work surface and very gently knead the citron into it, just until the citron is well incorporated.

6. Return the dough to a clean, well-buttered bowl and coat it with butter as before. Cover the bowl and let the dough rise for 45 minutes to 1 hour, or until it doubles in size.

7. Punch the dough down in the bowl, then transfer it to the work surface, and shape it into a 14- to 16-inch-long cylinder. Press the pecan half into the dough so it is completely encased. Place the cylinder on a buttered and floured cookie sheet and shape it into a ring by twisting and then overlapping the ends securely. Brush the entire surface of

the cake with the beaten egg yolk and let the cake rise again for about 1 hour, or until it doubles in size.

8. Preheat the oven to 375°.

9. Bake the cake on a rack in the middle of the oven for 35 to 45 minutes, or until it is golden brown. Transfer the cake to a wire rack to cool.

Decoration

$\frac{3}{4}$ *cup granulated sugar*
Green, purple, and yellow
  food coloring pastes
  (available in specialty
  food shops)
2 cups confectioners' sugar
3 tablespoons lemon juice
2 to 4 tablespoons water
$\frac{1}{4}$ *cup candied cherries*

1. Divide the granulated sugar into three $\frac{1}{4}$-cup batches and put each in a medium-sized bowl. Using a toothpick, place a tiny dot of green color paste on the palm of your hand. Sprinkle about 1 tablespoon of sugar from one batch over the paste, rub your palms together until the sugar turns evenly green, and return the sugar to the bowl from which it came. Now, blend the sugar together until you create an even shade of green without dark or light spots. Wash your hands and repeat this process to make the purple and yellow sugar.

2. Combine the confectioners' sugar, lemon juice, and 2 tablespoons of the water in a large bowl and beat with a wire whisk until the icing is smooth. If the icing is too stiff to spread with a metal spatula, beat in additional water. Spread the icing over the cake, letting any excess run down the sides. While the icing is still wet, sprinkle the colored sugar over the cake without overlapping the colors, creating three large spots of color. Decorate with the candied cherries.

German Butter Cake

Cake

YIELD: ONE 11½-BY-16-INCH CAKE

1 package active dry yeast
½ teaspoon, plus ¼ cup, granulated sugar
1 cup milk, brought to a boil and cooled to lukewarm (110°F to 115°F)
4 to 4½ cups all-purpose flour
¼ teaspoon salt
2 teaspoons grated lemon rind
8 tablespoons unsalted butter (1 stick)
3 large egg yolks

1. Butter an 11½-by-16-inch jelly-roll pan.

2. Stir the yeast and the ½ teaspoon sugar into the lukewarm milk. Let the mixture stand until it foams, about 4 to 6 minutes.

3. In a large bowl, combine the remaining ¼ cup sugar, 4 cups of the flour, the salt, lemon rind, butter, egg yolks, and yeast mixture. Stir all the ingredients together until the milk is absorbed by the flour. Remove the dough from the bowl and place it on a lightly floured surface.

4. Knead the dough by pushing it forward and folding it back in half on top of itself. Continue to knead the dough for 15 to 20 minutes, or until it is smooth and elastic. Sprinkle the dough, when necessary, with enough flour to keep it from sticking to your hands or the work surface.

5. Place the dough in a large buttered bowl and turn it to coat it with butter. Cover the dough with plastic wrap or a towel and let it rise for about 1 hour, or until it doubles in size.

6. Punch the dough down in the bowl, coat it with butter as before, cover, and let it rise for the second time until double in size.

7. Transfer the dough from the bowl to the work surface and press it flat with the palms of your hands. Lift the dough onto the prepared jelly-roll pan and press it into the sides and corners. Don't worry if the fit is not perfect; the dough will rise into place. Cover the dough with a towel and let it rise for 45 minutes or until doubled in size.

8. Preheat the oven to 375°.

Topping

½ pound unsalted butter (2 sticks)
¾ cup granulated sugar
½ teaspoon vanilla extract

1. In a small bowl, mix the butter, sugar, and vanilla together until they are well blended.

2. With your fingertips, make indentations all over the surface of the dough; these will act as wells for the butter. Dot

the dough with the entire butter mixture. Place the cake on a rack in the middle of the oven and bake for 35 to 40 minutes or until it is light gold and the sugar has crusted. Transfer the cake from the pan to a wire cake rack to cool.

Baking Powder Biscuits

YIELD: 24 BISCUITS

$4\frac{1}{2}$ *cups all-purpose flour*
3 tablespoons double-
  acting baking powder
$2\frac{1}{2}$ *teaspoons salt*
$1\frac{1}{2}$ *cups vegetable*
  shortening
$1\frac{1}{2}$ *cups milk*
4 tablespoons unsalted
  butter, melted

1. Lightly butter a large cookie sheet.

2. Preheat the oven to 400°.

3. Into a large bowl, sift together the flour, baking powder, and salt. Add the shortening and, with your fingers, rub the ingredients together until the mixture resembles large granules. Add the milk and, with a wooden spoon, stir the ingredients until they form a dough.

4. Transfer the dough to a lightly floured work surface and knead it until all the ingredients are well combined.

5. Roll the dough out to a thickness of $\frac{1}{2}$ inch (any shape will do). Cut out the biscuits with a round 2-inch cookie cutter and place them on the prepared baking sheet. Gather the scraps of dough into a ball, roll out the dough again, and cut more biscuits. Repeat until all the dough is used up.

6. Brush the tops of the biscuits with the melted butter, then place the biscuits on a rack in the middle of the oven and bake for 15 to 20 minutes, or until they are a delicate golden brown color. Serve warm.

CAKES, BREADS, AND TARTS

Stocking Stuffers

One of my favorite Christmas customs is that of filling up a big stocking with small gifts. I think that stocking presents should be for young and old alike. I love the sight of a candy cane poking out of a stocking top, and I still enjoy finding a beautiful orange in my stocking—a tradition dating back to when fresh fruit in winter was a real treat.

Candies such as the ones in this chapter make delightful stocking stuffers. Wrapped in cellophane, foil, or pieces of leftover Christmas paper, they make delicious additions to other miniature-sized gifts. Two of the recipes, those for marzipan and fondant, lend themselves to variations. Although the marzipan recipe tells you how to create fruits and vegetables out of this pliable confection, the shapes you can make are unlimited. Children especially love to join in and contribute their own designs. The fondant candies here are only two of many possibilities that use a fondant base.

Most of the following recipes were passed on to me by my friend Genevieve Youngerman of Clear Lake, Iowa. She first learned to make these candies in grade school in 1925, and I enjoy the thought that by passing her recipes on to you I am continuing yet another Christmas tradition.

Divinty

YIELD: ABOUT 1½ POUNDS

2½ cups granulated sugar
½ cup light corn syrup
1 cup water
2 large egg whites
1 teaspoon vanilla extract
1 cup chopped walnuts or
   pecans
½ cup candied cherries,
   halved

1. Place the sugar, corn syrup, and water in a 1-quart saucepan with straight sides. Cook the mixture over low heat until the sugar dissolves. Place a candy thermometer in the saucepan and bring the mixture to a boil over high heat. Continue to boil the syrup until the candy thermometer registers 172°.

2. With an electric mixer, beat the egg whites until they are firm. Add the syrup in a thin stream, continuing to beat until the egg whites are very thick. Add the vanilla and stir in the nuts and candied cherries. Drop the batter by the tablespoonful onto wax paper and let it stand for about 30 minutes, or until firm. If the divinty becomes too stiff to drop from a spoon, beat in a few drops of hot water.

Caramel Popcorn Balls

YIELD: ABOUT 12 BALLS

⅔ cup granulated sugar
⅔ cup brown sugar
¼ cup white corn syrup
⅓ cup water
Pinch salt
2 tablespoons butter, cut
   into small bits
6 cups freshly popped
   popcorn

1. Lightly grease a large bowl with vegetable oil and set it aside.

2. Place the granulated sugar, brown sugar, corn syrup, water, and salt in a 1-quart, straight-sided saucepan. Cook the mixture over low heat until the sugar dissolves. Place the candy thermometer in the saucepan and bring the mixture to a boil over high heat. Boil the syrup until it registers 305°. Remove the saucepan from the heat and carefully stir in the butter.

3. Place the popcorn in the bowl, and immediately pour the hot syrup over it. With a wooden spoon quickly mix them together.

4. As soon as the mixture is cool enough to handle, but still warm, shape the popcorn into 2-inch balls. If you are not a fast worker it would be advisable to preheat the oven to 300°. Then, if the caramel cools and becomes difficult to handle, you can put it in the oven to soften a bit, and continue to shape the balls.

Mixed Nut Crunch

YIELD: ABOUT 2 POUNDS

1½ cups granulated sugar
1 cup white corn syrup
¾ cup water
4 tablespoons unsalted
  butter
1½ teaspoons baking soda
1 cup blanched almonds,
  toasted
1 cup filberts, blanched and
  toasted

1. Lightly grease a jelly-roll pan with vegetable oil.

2. Place the granulated sugar, corn syrup, and water in a 1 quart saucepan with straight sides, and stir the mixture over low heat until the sugar dissolves. Place a candy thermometer in the saucepan, and bring the mixture to a boil over high heat. Boil the syrup until it registers 305° on the thermometer. Remove the saucepan from the heat and carefully stir in the butter, baking soda, almonds, and filberts.

3. Pour the mixture onto the jelly-roll pan, and when the nut crunch has cooled to room temperature, break it into small pieces.

Candied Grapefruit Peel

YIELD: ABOUT 48 PIECES

3 large grapefruits
2 cups granulated sugar
¾ cup water

1. Cut the grapefruits in half and squeeze them of their juice; store the juice in the refrigerator for another use.

2. Cut each grapefruit half into 4 pieces. With a paring knife, pull the white pith and flesh from the yellow peel and discard. Slice the peel into ⅓- to ½-inch-wide strips.

3. In a medium-sized saucepan, combine 1½ cups of the sugar and the water. Cook over low heat until the sugar has dissolved. Bring the syrup to a boil and add half of the grapefruit peel. Boil the peel for about 30 minutes, or until it is translucent. Remove the saucepan from the heat and, with a pair of tongs, remove the peel from the syrup, letting the excess syrup drip back into the saucepan. Place the cooked peel on a rack over a jelly-roll pan. Cook the remaining peel in the same manner.

4. When all the grapefruit peel has been cooked and cooled to room temperature, roll the pieces in the remaining ½ cup of granulated sugar.

Marzipan Fruit

Because of its texture and nonsticking quality, marzipan is very easy to model into fruits and vegetables. It is best to have the natural fruit and vegetables on hand for shape and color reference. If what you choose to shape is not in season, a color photograph can be very helpful.

You will find that wooden matches, toothpicks, and chopsticks will come in very handy for doing any detail work. There also are a few modeling tools available that professionals use to shape the various pieces. The fruits and vegetables can be colored with liquid food coloring and shaped in either their natural size or in miniature, depending on what your needs are. The larger pieces are best for stocking stuffers and the miniatures are fun to serve after dessert with coffee.

Marzipan

YIELD: ENOUGH FOR
1 LIFE-SIZE FRUIT
OR 8 MINIATURES

8 ounces almond paste
2¼ cups confectioners'
sugar
1 egg white, beaten lightly

Blend the almond paste and sugar together. Add enough egg white to create the consistency of modeling clay.

Banana

Color the marzipan light yellow and roll it into the shape of a banana. Dissolve cocoa in a little water and, with a small paint brush, streak the banana with brown lines.

Pear

Color the marzipan green or brown-green and shape it into a pear. Make impressions on the bottom and top and, if you wish, make a stem with brown marzipan.

Apple

Color the marzipan light green or green-yellow. Shape into an apple and make an impression on top with a chopstick. Finish the apple with a brown stem and a green leaf.

Mushrooms

Color the marzipan red for the mushroom caps, shape the caps, and press an indentation on the underside of each one. Make the stems with natural-colored marzipan, shaping one end into a point, and insert the pointed end into the underside of a mushroom cap. Make little white dots on top of the caps with royal icing (see page 24).

Potato

Shape small new potatoes with the natural-colored marzipan, then roll them in dark cocoa and make the "eyes" by indenting the surface with the tip of a matchstick.

Strawberry

Color the marzipan red and shape it into a strawberry. Roll the berry in granulated sugar. Make the hull with green marzipan.

Peaches

Mix red and yellow coloring to create a peach color. Shape an oval and make an impression at the stem end and a crease across the impression and down one side of the peach with the side of a matchstick or chopstick.

Orange

Make a smooth ball of orange-colored marzipan; then press a piece of paper towel against the sides to create the texture of orange skin. Push a whole clove into the stem end of the orange.

Fondant Candies

Fondant

YIELD: ABOUT 2 CUPS,
ENOUGH FOR 100 CANDIES

2 cups granulated sugar
⅛ teaspoon cream of tartar
1 cup water

1. Lightly grease a jelly-roll pan with vegetable oil.

2. Combine all the ingredients in a small saucepan and cook over low heat until the sugar dissolves. While the syrup cooks, wash down the inside of the saucepan with a wet pastry brush to prevent crystalization.

3. Bring the syrup to a boil and cook until it reaches the soft ball stage, about 238° on a candy thermometer.

4. Pour the mixture onto the jelly-roll pan and, when it is nearly cooled to room temperature, beat it with a wooden spoon until it is creamy. Then knead it until it is smooth and soft. Allow the fondant to stand for 24 hours to ripen before using.

Fondant Mints

Melt 1 cup of the fondant in the top half of a mint extract double-boiler. If it seems too thick, beat in a little water. Flavor the fondant with mint extract and color with green food coloring to the taste and color desired. With a teaspoon, drop about 50 candies on wax paper and let them dry.

Chocolate-covered Fondant

With your hands and using a teaspoon, shape 1 cup of the fondant into 50 small round balls and let them dry for 1 hour on wax paper. Melt 1 pound bitter or sweet chocolate, as desired. Using a toothpick, spear and then dip each fondant ball into the melted chocolate; place the candy on wax paper to dry.

Canapés and Hors d'Oeuvres

There is quite a difference between having a few friends in for drinks and snacks and having a cocktail party. A cocktail party, aside from the more elaborate food it entails, is a time for people to mingle, not only enjoying old friends but making new ones. At my parties, to make certain that people circulate, I never have enough chairs, even if I have to hide some. I also recommend keeping track of expected guests and spacing the serving of food accordingly, remembering that even the inevitable late arrivals deserve to be fed well.

Most canapés and hors d'oeuvres are delicate and cannot be prepared very far in advance. However, of the recipes that follow, the irresistible roasted pecans can be made weeks ahead and frozen. The cream cheese mixture for the endive can be made two or three days before the party, and the curried chicken for the mushroom caps can be made a day ahead and refrigerated. One of my favorite ways to feed cocktail party guests is with a spread of cold seafood, like the one shown in the second color section. Seafood is my personal passion, and it demands little or no cooking.

The drink recipes in this chapter can all be doubled, tripled, or quadrupled, depending on your needs. For a refreshing drink without alcohol, I recommend half cranberry juice and half ginger ale, garnished with a sprig of mint and an orange slice. If you are serving champagne, don't forget that the biggest and best wine cooler in the house is a bathtub filled with ice.

Pickled Shrimp

Pickled shrimp should be made at least one day before serving. They will keep in the refrigerator for up to five days. Before serving, let the shrimp stand at room temperature for two hours.

YIELD: ABOUT 8 SERVINGS

2 pounds medium-sized
   shrimp
1½ teaspoons coarse salt
2 large yellow onions,
   peeled and sliced very
   thinly
4 lemons, sliced very thinly,
   with the rinds left on
1 cup loosely packed bay
   leaves
Salt
Freshly ground pepper
3 cups olive oil,
   approximately
2 tablespoons chopped
   parsley

1. Place the shrimp in a large saucepan and cover them with cold water. Place the saucepan over high heat and, when the water just starts to come to a boil, drain the shrimp in a colander. Immediately place the shrimp on several thicknesses of newspaper, and sprinkle them with 1½ teaspoons of coarse salt. Wrap the shrimp in the newspaper to steam for 10 minutes.

2. Remove the shrimp from the paper and peel and devein them.

3. Spread a layer of the sliced onions in a deep glass serving dish, top with a layer of the shrimp, and sprinkle with a little salt and a few grindings of pepper. Cover with a layer of sliced lemon, then add a layer of bay leaves. Repeat the layers, starting with the onions, until all the ingredients are in the serving dish. Pour enough olive oil in the dish to cover the contents. Let the pickled shrimp marinate in the refrigerator for at least 24 hours. Serve at room temperature, sprinkled with the chopped parsley.

Mignonette Sauce

This once little-known sauce is gaining in popularity with shellfish lovers. Served as an option to red cocktail sauce, it is very complementary not only to oysters but also to clams on the half shell.

YIELD: ABOUT 1 CUP

1 cup distilled white vinegar
1½ teaspoons salt
1 tablespoon freshly
   ground white pepper
3 tablespoons finely
   chopped shallots

Combine all the ingredients and stir them with a fork until the salt dissolves.

Crabmeat-Turnip Canapé

The idea for this canapé was given to me by Donald Bruce White, a friend and one of New York's finest caterers.

YIELD: 10 TO 12 CANAPÉS

1 large carrot
1 tablespoon mayonnaise
Pinch cayenne pepper
½ pound fresh cooked or canned lump crabmeat
2 large white turnips, peeled
1 hard-cooked egg yolk forced through a sieve

1. Scrape the carrot and, using a lemon zester, slice it into long threads.

2. Bring 2 cups of water to a boil in a small saucepan. Add the carrot threads and blanch for about 10 seconds. Refresh the carrot in a strainer under cold running water. Place the carrot threads on paper towels and set aside.

3. Mix the mayonnaise and cayenne pepper together, then very gently stir in the crabmeat. Cover with plastic wrap and place in the refrigerator.

4. If you have a mandoline slicer, cut the turnips into $\frac{1}{16}$-inch-thick slices with a wafflelike texture on each side. To do this, use the corrugated blade and turn the turnip 90 degrees between each cut. If you do not have a mandoline, just slice the turnips very thinly.

5. Place a dollop of the crabmeat mixture on the center of each turnip slice. Garnish with the sieved hard-cooked egg and the carrot threads. (See the first color section.)

Hot Clam and Cheese Canapés

YIELD: 32 CANAPÉS

8 slices white bread
8 ounces cream cheese, at room temperature
½ teaspoon finely chopped garlic
2 teaspoons Worcestershire sauce
One 7-ounce can chopped clams, well drained

1. Toast the bread and, while it is still warm, cut four rounds out of each slice with a 1½-inch biscuit cutter. Set aside to cool.

2. Preheat the broiler.

3. In a small bowl, cream the cheese and add all the remaining ingredients. With a small metal spatula, mound the toast rounds with the cheese-clam mixture and place the rounds on a cookie sheet. Broil the canapés until the tops are golden brown. Serve immediately.

Irresistible Roasted Pecans

3 cups shelled pecans
6 tablespoons unsalted
  butter, melted
1 tablespoon coarse salt
1 teaspoon freshly ground
  white pepper

1. Preheat the oven to 350°.

2. Place the pecans in a large, shallow roasting pan, pour the melted butter over them, and sprinkle with the salt and white pepper. Toss the pecans with a large metal spatula until they are evenly coated with the butter and seasonings.

3. Place the roasting pan on a rack in the middle of the oven and roast the nuts for 15 minutes, tossing them once or twice with the spatula.

4. Remove the pan from the oven and place it on a wire rack until the nuts cool to room temperature.

5. Transfer the nuts to a paper bag and shake the bag gently to absorb any excess butter.

Smoked Salmon-Cheese Spread

YIELD: 1 POUND

12 ounces cream cheese,
  softened
$\frac{1}{4}$ pound smoked salmon,
  chopped very fine
$\frac{1}{2}$ teaspoon freshly ground
  white pepper
Salt to taste
1$\frac{1}{2}$ teaspoons lemon juice
1 cup sour cream
$\frac{1}{4}$ cup heavy cream
2 tablespoons chopped
  chives

1. In a small bowl, cream the cheese with a wooden spoon. Add the salmon, white pepper, salt, and lemon juice. Continue to beat until the ingredients are well blended.

2. Place a large piece of plastic wrap over the top of a deep, 16-ounce bowl or mold. Pushing the plastic wrap into a lining for the container, pack the cheese mixture tightly inside. Cover with plastic wrap and refrigerate for 2 to 3 hours.

3. In a small bowl, combine the sour cream, heavy cream and chopped chives. Add salt and pepper to taste, cover, and refrigerate.

4. To serve, invert the cheese mixture onto a shallow dish, remove the plastic wrap, and spread the sour cream sauce around the base. Serve with dark bread.

Hot Cream and Anchovy Dip

YIELD: 1½ CUPS

3 cups heavy cream
3 tablespoons unsalted butter
1 teaspoon finely chopped garlic
6 flat anchovies, drained, rinsed under cold running water, and finely chopped
Freshly ground pepper to taste

1. In a small saucepan over medium heat, reduce the cream to 1½ cups.

2. Melt the butter in a 2- to 3-cup cooking and serving casserole. Add the garlic and chopped anchovies, and cook a few minutes over low heat. Add the reduced cream and bring the dip to a simmer to blend the flavors. Season with pepper.

3. Place the casserole on a hot tray and serve immediately with the raw vegetables of your choice.

Bay Scallop Ceviche

YIELD: 8 SERVINGS

2 pounds uncooked bay scallops
½ cup lemon juice
½ cup lime juice
½ teaspoon finely chopped garlic
½ teaspoon crushed hot pepper flakes
1 sweet red pepper, cut into very fine strips
1 tablespoon chopped fresh coriander, plus a few sprigs for garnishing

In a glass bowl, combine all the ingredients except the coriander sprigs, cover, and let the mixture marinate in the refrigerator for about 2½ hours stirring occasionally, or until the scallops turn very white. Serve in a large bowl or in individual scallop shells, garnished with sprigs of fresh coriander.

Onion Drums

YIELD: 24 SMALL
SANDWICHES

12 thin slices of white
    bread (page 46) or
    brioche (page 28)
$\frac{1}{2}$ cup mayonnaise,
    approximately (preferably
    homemade)
1 large red onion, peeled
    and thinly sliced
Freshly ground pepper
Salt
$\frac{3}{4}$ cup chopped parsley,
    approximately

1. Coat each slice of bread with mayonnaise and top 6 of the slices with the onion rings. Sprinkle lightly with pepper and salt. Place the remaining slices of bread on top, pressing gently to make 6 sandwiches.

2. Using a 1½-inch round biscuit cutter, cut out 4 round "drums" from each sandwich.

3. Roll the edge of each drum in mayonnaise to coat it lightly, then roll it in chopped parsley. Refrigerate the drums on a cookie sheet with a damp paper towel over them until served.

Endive Filled with Cream Cheese and Caviar

YIELD: APPROXIMATELY 24
FILLED ENDIVE LEAVES

8 ounces cream cheese, at
    room temperature
2 tablespoons onion juice,
    squeezed from freshly
    grated onions
$\frac{1}{8}$ teaspoon cayenne pepper
$\frac{1}{4}$ teaspoon salt
2 large heads Belgian
    endive
One 4-ounce jar red caviar

1. Mix the cream cheese, onion juice, cayenne pepper, and salt in a small bowl until well blended. Set aside.

2. With a sharp knife, cut off and discard the bottom ends of the endive and slice the endive in half lengthwise.

3. Separate the leaves, using the largest and firmest for filling and reserving the smallest for another use.

4. Place half of the cream cheese mixture at a time in a pastry bag fitted with a number 3 star tube.

5. Pipe the seasoned cream cheese down the center of the endive leaves.

6. Using a toothpick, transfer the caviar eggs from the jar, spacing several of them evenly along the center of the cream cheese on each leaf. Refrigerate until ready to serve.

Cucumber Boats with Shrimp

YIELD: 12 CUCUMBER BOATS

3 medium-sized cucumbers
1½ cups chicken broth,
fresh or canned
2 teaspoons unflavored
gelatin
12 medium-sized shrimp,
cooked
2 tablespoons finely
chopped celery
1 teaspoon chopped fresh
dill weed, plus 12 tiny
sprigs of fresh dill
1 tablespoon chopped
chives
¼ teaspoon salt
¼ cup mayonnaise,
approximately (preferably
homemade)
½ teaspoon lemon juice
Dash Tabasco sauce

1. Scrape the peel from the cucumbers and cut off the ends. Cut the cucumbers crosswise into ½-inch-thick rounds. With a melon baller, scoop out a shallow well from the center of each slice. Sprinkle the cucumber rounds lightly with salt and invert them on a cake rack to let some of their water drain off.

2. Pour ½ cup of the chicken broth into a small heatproof bowl and sprinkle the gelatin over the top. When the gelatin has softened, set the bowl in a pan of simmering water and stir over low heat until the gelatin dissolves. Remove the pan from the heat, stir the gelatin mixture into the remaining chicken broth, and set aside.

3. Peel and devein the shrimp, and cut off the tail plus ¼-inch of the meat of 12 shrimp for decorating the boats; set aside. Chop the rest of the shrimp meat into very small pieces.

4. Place the chopped shrimp in a small bowl and add the celery, chopped dill, chives, salt, and mayonnaise. Mix the ingredients together, then season them with the lemon juice and Tabasco sauce. Stir in 1 tablespoon of the gelatin liquid and set aside.

5. Pat the cucumber rounds dry with paper towels. Spoon the shrimp mixture into the centers, mounding it slightly. Press one shrimp tail on top of each mound, and place the boats on a wire rack set over a jelly-roll pan.

6. Place the chicken broth in a small bowl over ice and stir it gently with a spoon until it becomes syrupy. Spoon the aspic over the cucumber boats to coat them evenly, and place a tiny sprig of dill on each boat. Keep in the refrigerator until ready to serve.

Mushroom Caps Stuffed with Curried Chicken

1 cooked chicken breast,
  skinned and boned
  (about 6 ounces)
2 tablespoons finely
  chopped celery
2 tablespoons chopped
  chives
¼ cup mayonnaise,
  approximately (preferably
  homemade)
1 teaspoon curry powder
Salt and pepper to taste
12 large white mushroom
  caps
½ cup finely chopped
  walnuts

1. Cut the chicken breast into small pieces, then chop the pieces a few times.

2. In a small bowl, mix the chopped chicken, celery, chives, mayonnaise, curry powder, and salt and pepper. If the mixture seems too dry, add a little more mayonnaise.

3. Wipe the mushroom caps with damp paper towels.

4. Using a small spoon, stuff the mushroom caps with the chicken mixture, mounding the filling to create a slight dome.

5. Place the chopped walnuts in a shallow bowl and press the chicken mixture into the nuts. Place the mushroom caps on a plate and refrigerate until serving time.

Holiday Eggnog

8 egg whites
¼ cup sugar
8 egg yolks
3 cups heavy cream, chilled
4 teaspoons superfine sugar
2½ cups blended whiskey
8 ounces Jamaica rum
1½ cups cold milk
½ teaspoon freshly grated
  nutmeg
2 tablespoons grated lemon
  rind
2 tablespoons grated
  orange rind

1. In a large bowl, beat the egg whites with a wire whisk or electric beater until frothy. Gradually add the ¼ cup sugar, and continue beating until the egg whites form soft peaks when the beater is lifted.

2. In another large bowl, beat the egg yolks until they run off the beater in thick ribbons. With a large rubber spatula, fold the egg whites and yolks together thoroughly.

3. Beat the heavy cream with the 4 teaspoons superfine sugar until the cream holds soft peaks.

4. Gently pour the egg mixture and cream into a large punch bowl or storage container. Slowly add the whiskey, rum, and milk, beating gently all the while.

5. Grate about ½ teaspoon of the nutmeg over the top of the eggnog, then sprinkle with the lemon and orange rind. Chill for at least 2 hours before serving.

Mimosa

YIELD: 6 TO 8 SERVINGS

2½ cups chilled fresh orange
   juice
1 bottle chilled champagne

Pour equal quantities of orange juice and champagne into
each champagne or wine glass and serve.

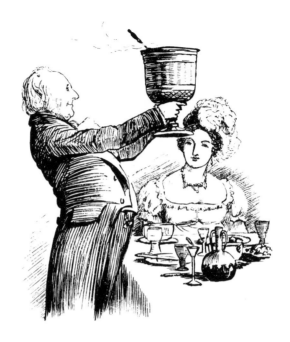

Champagne Punch

YIELD: 8 TO 10 SERVINGS

1 grapefruit
1 navel orange
1 pint strawberries, washed
   and then hulled
8 ounces brandy
8 ounces Benedictine
6 ounces maraschino
   liqueur
2 bottles chilled champagne
1 large bottle cold club
   soda

1. Section the grapefruit and orange, following the instructions for the orange segments in the curried shrimp recipe
on page 78. Place them in a medium-sized bowl, and add
the strawberries. Pour the brandy, Benedictine, and maraschino liqueur over the fruit. Refrigerate for 1 hour to let
the fruit macerate in the liqueurs.

2. Just before serving, fill a punch bowl with ice. Add the
fruit and macerating liquid, then the champagne and club
soda. Stir with a punch ladle and serve.

Wassail

In old England, wassail referred to several things: a toast to a person's health, a drink made with wine and spices served at Christmas time, revelry, and the singing of carols from house to house. My tenor friend, Dennis Williams, carries on the tradition by serving wassail, along with good food, at his tree trimming party each year, where carols are also part of the festivities. Dennis advises that you make sure the tree is completely trimmed before serving the first cup!

YIELD: 8 TO 10 SERVINGS

$\frac{1}{2}$ cup water
2 cups granulated sugar
1 teaspoon grated nutmeg
1 teaspoon ground ginger
Pinch ground mace
4 whole cloves
2 allspice berries, crushed
1 stick cinnamon
6 eggs, separated
1 bottle sherry
1 cup brandy

1. In a medium-sized saucepan, combine the water and sugar and place over low heat until the sugar dissolves. Add the nutmeg, ginger, mace, cloves, allspice, and cinnamon. Bring the mixture to a boil and let it boil for 5 minutes. Remove from the heat and strain; discard the contents of the strainer.

2. Beat the egg whites until they hold soft peaks. Beat the egg yolks until they are a light lemon-yellow in color.

3. In a large saucepan, heat the sherry and brandy until very hot.

4. In a large bowl and using a rubber spatula, fold the egg whites and yolks together thoroughly. Then stir in the spiced syrup.

5. With a wire whisk, slowly beat in the hot sherry and brandy and serve immediately.

Tom and Jerry

YIELD: 1 DRINK

$\frac{1}{2}$ cup milk
4 teaspoons unsalted butter
1 egg white
1 egg yolk
2 teaspoons granulated
  sugar
2 ounces brandy
2 ounces dark rum
Dash nutmeg

1. Place the milk and butter in a small saucepan and cook over low heat until the butter is melted.

2. In a small bowl, beat the egg white until it is very frothy. In another small bowl, beat the egg yolk with the sugar until it thickens slightly. Beat the egg white into the yolk mixture, then beat the egg into the hot milk. Add the brandy and rum. Return to low heat until the mixture is hot; do not let it boil. Pour the drink into a mug and sprinkle the top with nutmeg.

Hot Toddy

YIELD: 1 DRINK

$\frac{1}{4}$ teaspoon granulated
  sugar
1 lemon twist stuck with 1
  clove
1 small piece cinnamon
  stick
2 ounces bourbon
$\frac{3}{4}$ cup boiling water

Place the sugar, lemon twist, cinnamon stick, and bourbon in a mug. Pour in the boiling water and serve.

Hot Buttered Rum

YIELD: 1 DRINK

1 teaspoon granulated
  sugar
1 small piece cinnamon
  stick
2 ounces dark rum
2 teaspoons unsalted butter
$\frac{3}{4}$ cup hot milk
Dash nutmeg

Place the sugar, cinnamon stick, rum, and butter in a mug. Pour in the hot milk and sprinkle with a dash of nutmeg.

EDMUND EVANS

PART TWO

CHRISTMAS MENUS

Christmas Parties

Even though the Christmas party season starts in early December, time for entertaining always seems at a premium. Because of scarce space for large numbers of people or the desire to entertain separate groups—business associates, friends, or family for instance—two or three parties may be called for. One efficient solution is to give the parties two or three evenings in a row. Although I admit that this takes some stamina on your part, overall it limits the work considerably, especially if you use the same menu for each party. Party decorations and special serving dishes, borrowed if necessary, need only be assembled once, and one marketing trip may be all that is needed. Even with varying menus, there can be an economic advantage: food left over from the night before may be used for the second party. It's also economical to order liquor in bulk. In fact, overordering can be thrifty if your liquor store agrees you can return any unopened bottles.

Head starts are possible for both the menus suggested here. The cold lime soufflé for the shrimp curry dinner can be prepared two days ahead. The popadams can be fried a day in advance; if they aren't crisp enough at serving time, put them in a 400° oven for a few minutes. In the braised rabbit menu, the celery remoulade and the cranberry mousse can be made two days in advance. The rabbit can be made the day before and reheated in its casserole, and the creamed spinach can also be made a day ahead and reheated. While you are reheating the other dishes, make the crisp potato pancakes, which must be cooked at the very last minute.

```
┌─────────────────────────────────────────┐
│                 MENU                     │
│                                          │
│         Onion Drums (page 66)            │
│                                          │
│            Curried Shrimp                │
│                                          │
│             Boiled Rice                  │
│                                          │
│              Popadams                    │
│                                          │
│        Mixed Green Salad with            │
│    Garlic-flavored Vinaigrette Dressing  │
│                                          │
│           Cold Lime Soufflé              │
│                                          │
└─────────────────────────────────────────┘
```

Curried Shrimp

Highly spiced foods are supposed to be particularly suited to tropical climates, but I enjoy a curry dinner on any cold winter night. This curry has a French touch, and it is especially festive during the holiday season. Perhaps even better, it is so easy to organize that you will be able to spend most of your time with your guests. If you want to increase the recipe to serve 24 people, make half again the amount of sauce and add two and a half additional pounds of shrimp.

Many people frown at the thought of serving beer when entertaining, but if it is served well-chilled in a tall thin glass, it's the only drink I enjoy with curry. If you must serve wine, however, it should be a slightly sweet wine such as a Vouvray; a good dry white wine would be ruined by the spices in the curry powder.

YIELD: 10 TO 12 SERVINGS

4½ pounds medium-sized shrimp, peeled and deveined

2 teaspoons garlic, finely chopped

2 cups light cream or half-and-half

1. The day before serving, combine the shrimp, garlic, and cream in a large bowl. Stir, cover, and refrigerate overnight.

2. To make the sauce, drain and reserve the cream from the shrimp; return the shrimp to the refrigerator. Melt the butter in a large shallow pan over low heat. Add the onions and cook for about 5 minutes, or until soft but not brown. Stir in the curry powder and cook for 2 minutes longer. Gradually add the flour, stirring the mixture with a wooden

8 tablespoons butter (1 stick)

½ cup onions, finely chopped

3 tablespoons curry powder

1 cup flour

5 cups chicken broth, fresh or canned

spoon until it is smooth, and cook for 4 to 5 minutes. Remove the saucepan from the heat, and gradually add the chicken broth and then the reserved cream, beating the liquids into the flour mixture with a wire whisk. Return the saucepan to the heat and bring the sauce to a boil to thicken. Lower the heat and let the sauce simmer for 20 minutes.

3. Add the shrimp to the sauce one third at a time, stirring after each addition. Cook for 4 to 6 minutes, or until the shrimp are slightly firm.

4. Serve the curry in a large bowl or from a chafing dish, accompanied by boiled rice and the condiments that follow.

Condiments

3 cups grated unsweetened coconut (available in health food stores)

2 cups golden raisins

1 to 2 cups hot brandy or boiling water

3 cups prepared mango chutney

12 scallions

2 cups roasted peanuts, or substitute almonds, cashews, or macadamia nuts

3 large ripe bananas

1 tablespoon fresh lemon juice

6 eating oranges, preferably navel

1. To prepare the coconut, preheat the oven to 325°. Spread the coconut evenly on a large jelly-roll pan and place the pan on the middle rack of the oven. Toast the coconut for about 10 minutes, stirring occasionally, until it turns golden brown.

2. To prepare the raisins, bring the brandy or water to a boil, add the raisins, turn off the heat, and let the raisins sit for at least 1 hour, or until they have absorbed most of the liquid and are nice and plump.

3. Chutney usually needs to be chopped more finely before it is served. To do this, place the chutney in a large wire sieve set over a large bowl and press it with a wooden spoon to extract the juices. Reserve the juices. Transfer the solid pieces of chutney to a chopping board and, with a large lightly buttered knife, coarsely chop them. (Butter will keep the chutney from sticking to the knife.) Return the chopped chutney to the juices and refrigerate until ready to serve; it will keep indefinitely under refrigeration.

4. To prepare the scallions, wash them under cold running water a few hours before serving. With a knife, remove the root ends and cut off the tops, leaving about 2 inches of the green. Place 4 to 6 scallions at a time on a chopping board, and slice them crosswise into ¼-inch lengths. Place the chopped scallions in a dish, cover them with plastic wrap, and refrigerate until ready to serve.

5. Chop the nuts coarsely with a large kitchen knife or in a food processor. This can be done several days in advance.

6. Prepare the bananas a few hours before serving. First, peel the fruit, then cut it into $\frac{1}{2}$-inch-thick chunks. Place the banana pieces in a bowl and toss them with the lemon juice to keep them from discoloring. Cover the bowl tightly with plastic wrap.

7. Prepare the oranges by holding each one over a large bowl to catch the juices and, using a small, sharp knife, trim off the rind and white skin. Then cut down along the side of each membrane to free the sections in whole pieces, removing any seeds as you go along. Squeeze the membrane to extract the remaining juice. Cover and refrigerate the orange segments until ready to serve; if desired, they can be prepared a day in advance.

Boiled Rice

My first mentor was Rudolf Stanish, a very successful caterer, who taught me how to boil rice and keep it warm for a large group. Tuck a buttered piece of wax paper, buttered side down, over the rice. Keep the rice warm over very low heat, or in the oven set at the lowest temperature possible. I have kept rice hot in this manner for over an hour. Just before serving, stir in additional butter with a large kitchen fork.

YIELD: 10 TO 12 SERVINGS

4 cups long-grain rice
8 to 10 quarts of water
2 tablespoons salt
4 tablespoons unsalted butter, melted
Freshly ground pepper to taste

1. Put the water and salt in a large pot and, over high heat, bring the water to a rolling boil. Add the rice a little at a time so that the water never stops boiling. Boil the rice for 14 to 16 minutes. The rice should be tender but slightly firm when tested with your thumbnail against your index finger. Drain the rice in a colander and shake it a few times to rid it of excess water.

2. Return the rice to the pot and, over very low heat, fluff it up with a large kitchen fork. Continue to do this for a few minutes or until the rice dries out. Stir in the melted butter and freshly ground pepper to taste.

Popadams

YIELD: 12 SERVINGS

12 popadams (available in specialty food shops or East Indian markets)
Vegetable oil for deep-frying

1. Pour enough vegetable oil into a 9- to 10-inch skillet to fill it by two thirds. Heat the oil to 380° on a deep-fat frying thermometer.

2. One at a time, slide the popadams into the hot oil and, with a pair of metal tongs, press them down gently one or two times. Fry the popadams for about 2 to 3 minutes, then turn them and fry for an additional minute. They will inflate and become crisp. Transfer the popadams to paper towels to drain.

Mixed Green Salad with Garlic-flavored Vinaigrette Dressing

Salad

YIELD: 10 TO 12 SERVINGS

2 heads Belgian endive
2 heads Boston lettuce
1 head red lettuce
1 bunch watercress

1. With a small sharp knife trim the base of each endive, then wipe the endive clean with damp paper towels. Slice each endive in half lengthwise, then place the halves cut side down and slice them into very thin long strips.

2. Pick over the lettuce removing any damaged or wilted outer leaves. Wash the lettuce and watercress, drain them in a colander, and dry with paper towels or spin them dry in a salad drier. Store with the endive in the refrigerator until serving time.

Vinaigrette

$\frac{3}{4}$ cup olive oil
2 garlic cloves, peeled and crushed
4 teaspoons Dijon mustard
$\frac{1}{2}$ teaspoon salt
$\frac{1}{4}$ teaspoon freshly ground pepper, or to taste

1. Place the oil and garlic cloves in a small bowl and let them sit for 1 hour.

2. Discard the garlic, add all the remaining ingredients, and whisk them thoroughly together. Refrigerate until ready to serve. Before serving, mix the dressing well, then pour it over the greens. Toss the greens with a large fork and spoon until they are coated lightly with the dressing and serve.

Cold Lime Soufflé

YIELD: 10 TO 12 SERVINGS

1½ cups fresh lime juice
4 teaspoons unflavored
    gelatin
8 large egg yolks
1¾ cups granulated sugar
1½ cups evaporated milk
¼ cup finely grated lime
    peel
6 large egg whites

1. Wrap a lightly oiled sheet of doubled wax paper around the outside of a 1½-quart soufflé dish to make a collar. Secure the overlapping ends of the paper at the top with a few paper clips and tie the wax paper in place on the dish with string.

2. Pour the lime juice into a small heatproof bowl and add the gelatin. When the gelatin has softened, set the bowl in a shallow pan of simmering water and stir over low heat until the gelatin dissolves. Remove the pan from the heat, and set it aside, leaving the gelatin in the hot water.

3. Beat the egg yolks, then slowly add the sugar and continue beating until the yolks are thick enough to fall from the beater in a thick ribbon.

4. In a small saucepan, bring the milk to a boil, then remove it from the heat.

5. Resume beating the egg yolks while adding the hot milk in a thin stream. Return the milk mixture to the saucepan and, with a wooden spoon, stir over low heat until the mixture thickens to a custard that is just heavy enough to coat the spoon; do not let the mixture come to a boil. Remove the pan from the heat.

6. Stir in the gelatin and 3 tablespoons of the grated lime peel and transfer the custard to a large bowl to cool to room temperature.

7. When the custard has cooled, beat the egg whites until they form stiff but moist peaks. Stir about one fourth of the egg whites into the custard, then pour the custard over the remaining egg whites and fold them together gently but thoroughly. Pour the soufflé mixture into the prepared dish and refrigerate for 3 hours, or until set. Just before serving, gently remove the collar and sprinkle the top of the soufflé with the remaining lime peel.

Celery Remoulade

This wonderfully refreshing first course is served in many French restaurants. Because it is so light, it can be served with almost any menu.

YIELD: 8 TO 10 SERVINGS

3 large egg yolks, at room
    temperature
2 teaspoons Dijon mustard
1½ cups olive oil
¼ teaspoon salt
¼ teaspoon white pepper
4 teaspoons lemon juice
2½ pounds celery root

1. With a whisk or an electric mixer, beat the egg yolks with the mustard, salt, and pepper for 3 to 4 minutes, or until the egg yolks thicken.

2. Slowly incorporate 1 cup of the olive oil in a very fine stream. Continue to beat more rapidly until all the oil has been incorporated. Add the lemon juice and refrigerate.

3. With a vegetable peeler, remove the skin from the celery root. Cut the celery root into ⅛-inch-thick rounds, stack the rounds, and cut them into ⅛-inch-wide julienne strips.

4. Stir the remoulade sauce into the celery root and refrigerate for several hours before serving to let the flavors develop.

Rabbit Braised in Red Wine

One advantage to this dish is that, whether you use rabbit or chicken, it can be made a few days before you wish to serve it. Store it in the refrigerator in the same casserole it was cooked in and simply reheat it. Sometimes I garnish the serving platter with triangular-shaped toast points, and dip one point of each piece into the sauce and then into chopped parsley to give it some color.

YIELD: 8 TO 10 SERVINGS

6 tablespoons lard
$\frac{1}{2}$ pound salt pork, cut into $\frac{1}{4}$-inch dice
Two 2$\frac{1}{2}$- to 3-pound rabbits, cut into 8 pieces, or substitute the equivalent amount of chicken
Salt
Freshly ground pepper
1 cup flour
1 cup chopped onions
1 teaspoon finely chopped garlic
2 bay leaves
$\frac{1}{2}$ teaspoon thyme
$\frac{1}{4}$ cup brandy
$\frac{3}{4}$ cup dry red wine
3 cups chicken broth, homemade or canned
2 tablespoons chopped parsley

1. Melt the lard in a large skillet, add the salt pork, and cook until it is brown and crisp. Remove the salt pork with a slotted spoon and place it on paper towels to drain.

2. Season the rabbit with salt and pepper and dredge it in the flour, shaking off and reserving the excess. Brown the rabbit pieces in the fat remaining in the skillet, then transfer them to paper towels to drain.

3. Discard all but 3 tablespoons of the fat in the skillet. Add the onions and cook until lightly browned. Add the garlic to the onions and cook a few minutes longer.

4. Stir in the bay leaves, thyme, and 2 tablespoons of the flour used for dredging the rabbit. Cook for a few minutes, then add the brandy, red wine, and chicken broth, and simmer for about 5 minutes.

5. Place the rabbit pieces in a large casserole. Pour the red wine sauce over the rabbit, cover tightly, and cook the rabbit for 45 minutes to 1 hour, or until it is tender. Test for doneness with the tip of a paring knife. Garnish with the chopped parsley.

Creamed Spinach

YIELD: 8 TO 10 SERVINGS

*4 to 5 pounds fresh
    spinach
1½ teaspoons salt
6 tablespoons unsalted
    butter
2 tablespoons finely
    chopped onions
6 tablespoons flour
1 cup milk
½ cup heavy cream
¼ teaspoon freshly ground
    white pepper
¼ teaspoon freshly ground
    nutmeg*

1. Trim any tough stems from the spinach and pick off and discard any damaged or wilted leaves. Wash the spinach thoroughly, and place it in a large pot, packing it down if necessary. Sprinkle the spinach with 1 teaspoon of the salt and cook over very low heat, stirring occasionally, until the leaves are wilted. Drain the spinach in a colander and, when it is cool enough to handle, chop it finely with a large knife. Set the spinach aside.

2. To make the sauce, melt the butter in a small heavy saucepan. When the butter is hot, add the chopped onions and cook until they are translucent; do not let them color. Stir in the flour and cook for 2 minutes. Gradually whisk in the milk and cream, and bring the sauce to a boil to thicken. Reduce the heat, add the remaining ½ teaspoon of salt, the pepper, and the nutmeg and let the sauce simmer for 10 minutes.

3. Stir in the chopped spinach, and continue to cook for an additional 5 minutes. Taste for seasoning before serving.

Crisp Potato Pancakes

These lacy, crisp brown pancakes are not only delicious with the rabbit (or chicken) in wine sauce, but also make a wonderful lunch served with homemade apple sauce. However, I would not advise making these pancakes for more than ten people; keeping them warm too long robs them of much of their character.

YIELD: 8 TO 10 SERVINGS

*8 medium-sized baking
    potatoes, peeled
¼ cup finely chopped onion
3 teaspoons salt
¾ cup clarified butter*

1. Preheat the oven to 200°. Line a jelly-roll pan with paper towels.

2. Grate the potatoes on a four-sided grater, using the side with the large holes and pushing the potato against the grater with long strokes. Let the pieces fall into a large bowl. Toss the grated potatoes with the chopped onion and salt.

3. Heat the butter in a large sauté pan until it is very hot, then add about 2 tablespoons of the potato mixture at a

time for each pancake. As the potatoes fry, flatten them out into pancakes with a metal spatula. When the pancakes have browned on one side, turn and brown them on the other side. Transfer the pancakes to the jelly-roll pan and keep them warm in the oven while you cook the remaining potatoes.

Cranberry Mousse

YIELD: 8 TO 10 SERVINGS

4 envelopes unflavored gelatin
6 cups bottled cranberry juice
2½ cups fresh cranberries
2¼ cups granulated sugar
9 large egg whites
¾ teaspoon salt
2 cups heavy cream, chilled
1 tablespoon confectioners' sugar

1. Grease a 10-cup melon mold with vegetable oil.

2. Place the gelatin in a small heatproof bowl. Add ¾ cup of the cranberry juice. When the gelatin has softened, set the bowl in a pan of simmering water until the gelatin dissolves, remove the pan from the heat, and set it aside, leaving the bowl in the water.

3. Wash the cranberries and place them in a large saucepan with the remaining cranberry juice and 1½ cups of the granulated sugar. Bring to a boil over high heat, reduce the heat to low, and simmer the berries, uncovered, for about 5 minutes, or until the skins of the berries just pop. Drain the juice from the berries into a large heatproof bowl, add the gelatin, and refrigerate.

4. Reserve 8 of the largest whole, cooked berries for decorating the mousse, and chop the remaining berries with a knife.

5. When the cranberry-gelatin mixture becomes quite syrupy, beat the egg whites until they form soft peaks. Add the salt and the remaining sugar and continue to beat until the egg whites hold firm but moist peaks. Whip 1½ cups of the heavy cream at moderate speed until it holds firm but moist peaks. With a large rubber spatula, thoroughly fold the egg whites and whipped cream together. Fold the egg white-cream mixture into the thickened cranberry juice until no trace of white shows, then fold in the chopped berries. Pour the mousse into the prepared mold and cover. Refrigerate for about 6 hours, or until the mousse has set.

6. To unmold the mousse, dip the mold into hot water for just a few seconds. Dry the mold and remove the cover. Place a well-chilled inverted serving plate over the top of the mold, and with both hands, hold the plate and mold tightly together, then turn them over, and remove the mold.

7. Whip the remaining $\frac{1}{2}$ cup of heavy cream with the confectioners' sugar at moderate speed until it holds stiff peaks. Spoon the cream into a pastry bag fitted with a number 5 star tube. Pipe the cream onto the mousse (see the photograph in the first color section to guide you), and place the reserved whole berries at even intervals on top of the whipped cream.

Brunch

In 1974, when I was invited to Tokyo to teach a number of cooking classes, American brunch dishes were one of the most popular items on the curriculum because the Japanese were just getting interested in this Western manner of entertaining. Surprisingly, here in the United States many people have still to discover what a wonderful form of entertaining a brunch can be, especially on a Sunday. My guests are usually invited for noon and depart by midafternoon—or sometimes earlier if they are on their way to a museum or a concert. This leaves me with the rest of the day to relax before the start of a busy week.

Brunch can be as formal or informal as you wish. I enjoy being informal to the extent that I make my guests their first drink and then arrange the bar so that they can help themselves to a second. Bloody Marys have long been the most popular brunch cocktail, but mimosas (page 69) are rapidly gaining favor. Another, more elegant option, is to serve only champagne.

Of the three menus suggested here, the finnan haddie roulade and the ratatouille egg cake work the best for large groups; they are easily served from a buffet and can be eaten standing up. The chicken livers in choux puff pastry work best for a small number of guests.

Remember that many people will skip breakfast in anticipation of brunch. Your guests will be hungry, so serve the food shortly after they arrive.

```
┌─────────────────────────────────────────┐
│                                         │
│              MENU                       │
│                                         │
│        Potato and Leek Soup             │
│                                         │
│     Chicken Livers and Mushrooms in     │
│           Choux Puff Pastry             │
│                                         │
│      Green Bean Salad (page 106)        │
│                                         │
│       Chestnut Bavarian Cream           │
│                                         │
└─────────────────────────────────────────┘
```

Potato and Leek Soup

Soup

YIELD: 6 TO 8 SERVINGS

*3 large leeks, with the root
    ends removed*
*2 pounds boiling potatoes,
    peeled and cut into
    quarters*
*2½ quarts chicken broth,
    fresh or canned*
¼ teaspoon white pepper
1 cup heavy cream

1. Cut the green tops from the leeks and set them aside for the garnish. Slice the white part of the leeks into ¼-inch rounds and wash them in a colander under cold running water.

2. Combine the leeks, potatoes, chicken broth, and white pepper in a 4- to 6-quart saucepan. Place the pan over high heat and bring the broth to a boil. Reduce the heat to low and simmer the soup, half covered, until all the vegetables are soft.

3. Strain the contents of the saucepan into another pot or large heatproof bowl.

4. Place the strained solids in a food processor or blender and puree them. Return the vegetable mixture and the broth to the original saucepan. Add the heavy cream, stir well and bring to a boil. Taste for seasoning and remove from the heat. For an extra-smooth soup, strain again, pushing any bits of leek and potato through the strainer with the back of a wooden spoon. Serve with a garnish of carrot and leek strips.

Garnish

1 large carrot
The green tops of the leeks

1. Scrape the carrot and, using a lemon zester, cut 2-inch-long carrot threads. Cut the green part of the leeks crosswise into 2-inch lengths, then cut lengthwise into fine strips.

2. Bring 2 cups of water to a boil in a small saucepan, add the carrot threads and blanch for about 10 seconds. Refresh the carrots in a strainer under cold running water. Cook the leek strips in the same fashion for about 4 to 6 minutes, or until tender. Refresh under cold water and combine with the carrots.

3. Place the carrots and leeks in a heated tureen and pour the hot soup over them, or, if you prefer, scatter the garnish over the top of the soup.

Chicken Livers and Mushrooms in Choux Puff Pastry

Filling

YIELD: 6 TO 8 SERVINGS

1 pound chicken livers
6 tablespoons unsalted butter
¼ cup finely chopped shallots
1½ cups sliced mushrooms
4 teaspoons flour
1 cup chicken broth, fresh or canned
2 large tomatoes, peeled, seeded, and coarsely chopped
Salt and freshly ground pepper to taste

1. Separate the chicken livers into halves and trim off any fat.

2. Heat the butter in a large skillet until it is very hot but not brown. Add the chicken livers and sauté them, stirring with a slotted spoon until they are nicely browned. Remove the livers from the pan and set them aside.

3. Add the shallots to the butter remaining in the skillet and cook for a few seconds. Stir in the mushrooms and cook for 3 to 4 minutes. Stir in the flour, broth, and chopped tomatoes. Season with salt and pepper, and simmer the sauce for 5 minutes. Set aside.

Pastry

2 cups water
½ teaspoon salt
12 tablespoons unsalted butter (1½ sticks)
2 cups all-purpose flour, sifted
8 large eggs
2 egg yolks, beaten

1. Preheat the oven to 400°.

2. Place the water, salt, and butter in a medium-sized saucepan and bring to a boil. Remove the saucepan from the heat and add the flour all at once. Beat the flour mixture with a large wooden spoon until the dough leaves the sides of the pan. Return the pan to medium heat, and heat the mixture for 1 minute. Remove the pan from the heat and let the dough sit for 5 minutes. Beat in the 8 eggs two at a

time, then continue to beat until the pastry is smooth and shiny.

3. Divide the pastry into eight equal portions. Lightly butter eight oven-proof serving dishes that are about 4 inches in diameter and $2\frac{1}{2}$ to 3 inches deep. Line each dish with a portion of the pastry by pressing it against the dish with your fingers. Brush the pastry with the beaten egg yolk, and place the dishes on a large cookie sheet.

4. Divide the chicken livers and sauce evenly among the dishes and bake on a rack in the middle of the oven for 35 to 40 minutes, or until the pastry is nicely puffed.

Chestnut Bavarian Cream

YIELD: 6 TO 8 SERVINGS

½ cup water
2 tablespoons, plus 1
  teaspoon, unflavored
  gelatin
1½ cups milk
6 large egg yolks
1½ cups granulated sugar
1½ teaspoons vanilla
1½ cups unsweetened
  chestnut pureé
1 ounce semisweet
  chocolate, melted
2¼ cups heavy cream
¼ cup dark rum
Grated semisweet chocolate
  (optional)

1. Lightly oil a 6-cup mold.

2. Pour the water into a small heatproof bowl and sprinkle the gelatin over it. When the gelatin has softened, set the bowl in a pan containing a shallow amount of simmering water and stir over low heat until the gelatin dissolves. Remove the pan from the heat and leave the bowl of gelatin in the water.

3. Bring the milk to a boil and set it aside.

4. Beat the egg yolks, then slowly add the sugar. Continue beating until the yolks are thick enough to fall in a thick ribbon when the beater is lifted.

5. Continue to beat the egg yolk mixture while adding the hot milk in a thin stream. Return the milk mixture to the saucepan and, with a wooden spoon, stir over low heat until the mixture thickens to a custard that is just heavy enough to coat a spoon. Do not let the mixture come to a boil or it will curdle. Remove the pan from the heat.

6. Stir in the gelatin, vanilla, chestnut pureé, and melted chocolate. Continue to stir until all the ingredients are well blended. Strain the mixture into a large bowl and let it cool to room temperature.

7. Whip the heavy cream until it forms firm but moist peaks. Beat in the rum. Fold one-third of the whipped cream into the chestnut mixture, then pour the chestnut mixture over the remaining cream, and fold them together gently but thoroughly. Pour the Bavarian cream into the prepared mold. Refrigerate the Bavarian for 3 to 4 hours, or until set.

8. To unmold the Bavarian, dip the mold into hot water for a few seconds, then dry the mold. Invert a well-chilled serving plate over the top of the mold and, with both hands holding the plate and mold together tightly, turn them over and remove the mold. If you like, decorate the top with grated semisweet chocolate.

```
┌─────────────────────────────────────────────┐
│                                             │
│                  MENU                       │
│            Consommé Bellevue                │
│           Ratatouille Egg Cake              │
│          Open-faced Apple Tart              │
│                                             │
└─────────────────────────────────────────────┘
```

Consommé Bellevue

Don't let the combination of clam juice, chicken broth, and whipped cream deter you from enjoying this fabulous and wonderfully light soup.

YIELD: 6 TO 8 SERVINGS

1½ quarts chicken broth,
    fresh or canned
1 quart clam juice
1 teaspoon finely chopped
    garlic
½ teaspoon freshly ground
    white pepper
½ cup chilled heavy cream,
    whipped with a pinch of
    salt
8 to 10 thin slices of lemon
2 tablespoons finely
    chopped parsley

1. Combine the chicken broth, clam juice, garlic, and white pepper in a 3- to 4-quart saucepan. Bring to a boil over high heat, reduce the heat and let the consommé simmer for 20 minutes.

2. Strain the soup through a strainer that is lined with a double thickness of damp cheesecloth into another saucepan.

3. Just before serving, bring the soup to a boil to heat it. Serve it in bouillon cups, garnished with a dollop of the whipped cream, 1 slice of lemon, and a sprinkling of the parsley.

Ratatouille Egg Cake

This colorful ratatouille egg cake is at its best when served at room temperature. Sliced in wedges and sprinkled with Parmesan cheese, it makes a perfect brunch dish that can be prepared hours in advance. It is also delicious as an accompaniment to roast leg of lamb.

The ratatouille itself is usually thought of during late summer or early fall, but it can very successfully be made with canned tomatoes and dried basil any time of the year. The important thing to remember, whatever the season, is that ratatouille is best if allowed to mellow in the refrigerator for two days before serving. As with coleslaw, potato salad, and baked beans, I always make ratatouille in generous quantities because it is wonderful to serve as an accompaniment to leftovers or to have on hand for unexpected guests. With this recipe, you will have enough ratatouille for the egg cake as well as for serving at another time.

Ratatouille

YIELD: 10 TO 12 CUPS

2 large yellow onions, peeled and very coarsely chopped

2 medium-sized eggplants, cut into 1-inch cubes

4 medium-sized zucchini, sliced into $\frac{1}{3}$-inch-thick rounds

1 large green pepper, seeded and cut into $\frac{1}{2}$-inch dice

1 large red pepper, seeded and cut into $\frac{1}{2}$-inch dice

6 very ripe tomatoes, blanched, peeled, seeded, and coarsely chopped

1$\frac{1}{2}$ teaspoons finely chopped garlic

4 teaspoons dried, or $\frac{1}{4}$ cup fresh, basil

2 teaspoons salt

$\frac{1}{2}$ teaspoon freshly ground pepper

$\frac{1}{2}$ cup olive oil

$\frac{1}{2}$ cup chopped flat-leaf parsley

1. Preheat the oven to 350°.

2. Place all the vegetables in a large ovenproof casserole, season with garlic, dried basil (if you are using it), salt, and pepper, and pour the oil over them. Mix the vegetables with a large spoon to coat them completely with the oil. Cover the casserole, place it on the rack in the middle of the oven, and bake the vegetables for 1$\frac{1}{2}$ hours. Remove the cover and continue to bake the ratatouille for an additional 15 to 30 minutes, or until most of the liquid has evaporated. Remove the casserole from the oven and, when the ratatouille has cooled to room temperature, stir in the fresh basil (if you are using it) and parsley.

Egg Cake

YIELD: 6 TO 9 SERVINGS

12 large eggs
$\frac{1}{4}$ teaspoon salt
$\frac{1}{4}$ cup water
6 to 8 tablespoons butter
$3\frac{1}{2}$ cups ratatouille, at room temperature

1. With a wire whisk, beat the eggs, salt, and water together in a large bowl until well blended. Pour the mixture through a fine wire sieve into another bowl.

2. Heat 2 tablespoons of the butter in an 8- to 9-inch skillet over high heat until the butter is very hot but not brown. Reduce the heat to medium, and pour one-fourth of the egg mixture into the pan. Let the egg mixture cook until it sets and turns light brown on the bottom; lift the edge with a metal spatula to check it. Turn the layer of egg over, and cook it for about 1 minute on the other side. Slide the egg layer onto a large plate. Repeat the same process, using as much butter as necessary to keep the skillet well greased, until you have 4 layers of egg.

3. Place one layer of egg on a large serving plate and spread it evenly with 1 cup of the ratatouille. Repeat until all the egg layers are used, mounding the last one with $\frac{1}{2}$ cup of the ratatouille.

Open-Faced Apple Tart

YIELD: 8 SERVINGS

1½ cups all-purpose flour
3 tablespoons, plus ¼ cup,
    granulated sugar
1 egg yolk
1 hard-cooked egg yolk,
    sieved
12 tablespoons unsalted
    butter (1½ sticks),
    softened
2 teaspoons finely grated
    lemon rind
4½ pounds Granny Smith
    or green Golden
    Delicious apples
½ cup water
6 tablespoons fresh lemon
    juice
¾ cup apricot preserves,
    heated and strained

1. In a large bowl and with your hands, work the flour, 3 tablespoons of the sugar, both egg yolks, the butter, and lemon rind together into a mass. Continue to work the pastry until the ingredients are well blended; no streaks of egg yolk should show. Wrap the pastry in plastic wrap and refrigerate for at least 1 hour.

2. Reserve 2 of the largest apples for the top of the tart and peel, core, and cut the remaining apples into 1-inch-thick slices. Place the sliced apples in a heavy saucepan with the ¼ cup of sugar, the water, and 4 tablespoons of the lemon juice. Cover the saucepan tightly and cook the apples over low heat for 10 minutes. Remove the cover, raise the heat, and continue to cook the apples until the liquid evaporates. Add additional sugar to taste, scrape the apple mixture into a bowl, and let it cool to room temperature.

3. Remove the pastry from the refrigerator and roll it out between two pieces of wax paper until it is a little more than ⅛-inch thick. Peel off the top piece of wax paper, then pick up the bottom piece and invert the pastry over a 10-inch tart pan with a removable bottom. Peel off the paper, and gently fit the pastry into the bottom and sides of the pan. Push the rolling pin across the top of the pan to remove any excess pastry. Place the pastry shell in the refrigerator.

4. Preheat the oven to 450°.

5. Peel and core the 2 remaining apples and cut them into 1/16-inch-thick slices. Remove the tart shell from the refrigerator and fill it with the cooled apple mixture. Make concentric circles with the thinly sliced apples by slightly overlapping the slices until the entire surface of the tart has been covered. Brush the sliced apples with the remaining 2 tablespoons of lemon juice and bake on a rack in the middle of the oven for about 50 minutes, or until the sliced apples take on a golden-brown edge. Remove the tart from the oven and place on a wire rack to cool to room temperature.

6. Warm the strained apricot preserves and, with a pastry brush, gently glaze the top of the tart.

```
┌─────────────────────────────────────┐
│                                     │
│              MENU                    │
│                                     │
│         Pickled Mushrooms            │
│                                     │
│     Finnan Haddie Roulade with       │
│           Mustard Sauce              │
│                                     │
│           Endive Salad               │
│                                     │
│   German Butter Cake (pages 52–53)   │
│                                     │
└─────────────────────────────────────┘
```

Pickled Mushrooms

YIELD: 6 TO 8 SERVINGS

1 cup olive oil
1 cup vegetable oil
½ cup dry white wine
½ teaspoon dry red pepper flakes, crushed
2½ teaspoons salt
¼ cup finely chopped onion
2 teaspoons finely chopped garlic
2 bay leaves
1½ pounds small mushrooms
¼ cup flat-leaf parsley, chopped
6 to 8 lemon wedges

1. Combine the olive and vegetable oils. In a large mixing bowl, beat together the oil, white wine, pepper flakes, and salt. Add the onion and garlic and beat until well blended. Add the bay leaves.

2. Wipe the mushrooms clean with dampened paper towels. Slice off the ends of the mushroom stems, drop the mushrooms into the marinade, and stir to coat them evenly. Cover with plastic wrap and refrigerate for 3 days before serving.

3. Just before serving, mix in the chopped parsley. Serve on a bed of lettuce with the lemon wedges.

Finnan Haddie Roulade with Mustard Sauce

The roulade in this recipe is actually a kind of fallen cheese soufflé. Rolled around the smoked haddock filling, it is a perfect brunch dish for either small or large groups. The recipe can be doubled, tripled, or quadrupled, depending on the number of guests you intend to serve. Have the roulades rolled and ready for the oven before the first guest arrives; heating will take only minutes. If making several roulades for a large group seems to be too much to handle, simply prepare the finnan haddie, put it in a large saucepan, pour all the sauce into the pan, reheat the mixture, and serve it in commercial patty shells. You may also serve the finnan haddie au gratin from a large casserole. Sprinkle the top with bread crumbs and Parmesan cheese, dot it with butter, and bake the casserole in the oven at 375° for 20 to 30 minutes, or until the finnan haddie is bubbly hot and the top is crusty. Or you can simply serve the finnan haddie with rice. Whatever you decide to do, your guests are sure to enjoy this delicately smoked fish.

Finnan Haddie

YIELD: 6 TO 8 SERVINGS

2 pounds smoked haddock
1 medium-sized onion, sliced
½ teaspoon freshly ground white pepper
3 cups milk, approximately

1. Place the smoked haddock in a large skillet and scatter the sliced onions on top. Sprinkle with the white pepper and add enough milk to just cover the fish. Bring the milk to a boil over high heat, reduce to a simmer, and cook the haddock partially covered for 10 minutes, or until the fish flakes easily when pulled with a fork.

2. With a slotted spatula, transfer the cooked fish to a large plate. Discard the onions, cover the fish with plastic wrap, and set it aside.

The Roulade

4 tablespoons unsalted butter, softened
⅔ cup grated Parmesan cheese
3 tablespoons flour
1 cup milk
½ teaspoon salt
⅛ teaspoon cayenne pepper
4 egg yolks, beaten
6 egg whites

1. Line a 17½-by-11-inch jelly-roll pan with wax paper. Coat the paper with 1 tablespoon of the softened butter and sprinkle it with 2 tablespoons of the Parmesan cheese.

2. Preheat the oven to 400°.

3. Melt the 3 remaining tablespoons of butter in a small saucepan, add the flour, and cook over low heat, stirring with a wooden spoon, for 2 minutes. Gradually add the milk, beating with a wire whisk until it comes to a boil and the mixture is smooth and thick. Remove the pan from the

heat and beat in the salt, cayenne pepper, the beaten egg yolks, and finally the remaining Parmesan cheese. Set aside.

4. Beat the egg whites until stiff, then beat one quarter of the whites into the cheese mixture. Pour the sauce mixture over the remaining egg whites and fold them together gently and thoroughly. Pour the mixture onto the prepared jelly-roll pan, and with a rubber spatula, spread the mixture evenly. Place the pan on a rack in the middle of the oven and bake the roulade for 15 minutes, or until it has risen and is firm to the touch.

Mustard Sauce

3 tablespoons unsalted
  butter
3 tablespoons flour
$1\frac{1}{2}$ cups milk
1 cup heavy cream
3 teaspoons Dijon mustard
$1\frac{1}{2}$ teaspoons dry mustard
$\frac{3}{4}$ teaspoon salt
Freshly ground white
  pepper to taste
$1\frac{1}{2}$ teaspoons distilled white
  vinegar
2 tablespoons capers
2 pimentos, cut into $\frac{1}{4}$-inch-
  wide strips

1. Melt the butter in a medium-sized saucepan. Add the flour and cook over low heat, stirring with a wooden spoon, for 2 minutes.

2. Gradually add the milk and heavy cream, beating with a wire whisk until the sauce thickens and is smooth. Beat in the Dijon and dry mustard, salt, and pepper.

3. Remove from the heat and stir in the vinegar, capers, and pimento.

Assembling the Roulade

1. Flake the fish into a bowl and stir in 1 cup of the hot sauce to reheat and bind the haddock. Spoon the fish along one long edge of the roulade. Using the wax paper as an aid, roll the roulade jelly-roll fashion around the fish.

2. With both hands, lift the roulade onto the jelly-roll pan. Return the roulade to the oven for 10 minutes.

3. Serve the roulade on a large platter masked with the remaining sauce.

Endive Salad

Though expensive, this salad is pretty to look at and delicious to eat, and it will hold up a long while without wilting.

<u>YIELD: 6 TO 8 SERVINGS</u>

1 cup olive oil
3 tablespoons tarragon
   vinegar
2 teaspoons Dijon mustard
½ teaspoon salt
¼ teaspoon freshly ground
   white pepper
6 heads Belgian endive
¼ cup chopped parsley
¼ cup chopped chives
1 large tomato, blanched,
   peeled, seeded, and
   coarsely chopped
1 hard-cooked egg yolk,
   sieved

1. In a small bowl and with a fork, beat together the olive oil, tarragon vinegar, mustard, salt, and pepper. Set aside.

2. With a small sharp knife trim the base of each endive, then wipe it clean with damp paper towels. Slice the endive in half lengthwise, then place it cut side down, and slice it into very thin long strips.

3. In a large salad bowl, toss the endive strips with the salad dressing. Scatter the parsley, chives, tomato, and egg yolk on top and toss again.

Christmas Eve Buffet

Among my fondest Christmas food memories are those of family Christmas Eve buffets. Ours always consisted of an abundance of both hot and cold dishes. Although the selection varied from year to year, there was always one hot seafood dish, usually lobster Newburg, and there would always be some kind of roasted beef served at room temperature, along with various salads. I can't remember a Christmas without my mother's potato salad; the bowl she used was too large for the refrigerator and it always ended up, temptingly, on my bedroom window sill, with the window open a crack.

In addition to the seafood, beef, and salads, our Christmas Eve table displayed the beautiful cakes, cookies, and candies that had been prepared for the holidays. To them was always added a bowl of fresh fruits, carefully chosen for their colors as well as flavors.

The elements of the following menus may be combined to accommodate twenty or more guests. To the lobster Newburg menu add the turkey of the farm served at room temperature. Double the portions of rice pilaf, green bean salad, and the mushroom-filled puff pastry, and serve two of the strawberry cream rolls from the turkey of the farm menu. Arranged on a buffet decorated with pine boughs and holly, the result will be your own memorable meal.

```
┌─────────────────────────────────────────┐
│  ┌───────────────────────────────────┐  │
│  │              MENU                  │  │
│  │  Smoked Salmon-Cheese Spread (page 64)  │  │
│  │         Turkey of the Farm        │  │
│  │         Sautéed Snow Peas         │  │
│  │           Glazed Onions           │  │
│  │          Gratin Potatoes          │  │
│  │       Strawberry Cream Roll       │  │
│  └───────────────────────────────────┘  │
└─────────────────────────────────────────┘
```

Turkey of the Farm

If your Christmas day plans do not include turkey—for instance, if you are going to serve the traditional English roast beef dinner on pages 116–117—Turkey of the Farm is wonderful for a Christmas Eve buffet.

<u>YIELD: 8 TO 10 SERVINGS</u>

One 12-pound turkey, boned, with the skin left on
¼ cup, plus 2 tablespoons, unsalted butter
½ cup chopped shallots
1 teaspoon salt
½ teaspoon freshly ground pepper
2 teaspoons tarragon

1. Preheat the oven to 350°.

2. Place the turkey, skin side down, on the work surface. In a small bowl, mix the ¼ cup of butter together with the shallots, salt, pepper, and tarragon, then rub the mixture into the turkey flesh. Roll the turkey up jelly-roll fashion and secure it in several places with butcher cord.

3. Place the turkey on a rack in a shallow roasting pan and spread it with the remaining 2 tablespoons butter. Place the roasting pan on a rack in the middle of the oven, and roast the turkey for 2 to 2½ hours, or until the juice runs clear when the meat is tested with the tip of a paring knife.

4. Transfer the turkey to a warm platter, remove the butcher cord and let the turkey sit for 20 minutes before slicing.

Warming winter soup. *Leek and potato soup, topped with* ▶
colorful julienne strips of carrot and leek

A hearty Christmas breakfast. *From top to bottom: brioche, mimosas (champagne with orange juice), stollen, Swedish hash*

Facing page: New Year's day buffet. *From lower left, clockwise: pumpernickel and rye bread, raw vegetables with pesto mayonnaise, country pâté, pickled onions and olives, brie in brioche, cornichon pickles, mustard, duck pâté, croquembouche, baked ham with bourbon peaches, chicken liver pâté, smoked salmon, pickled halibut, cotechino sausage*

Gifts from the sea. *From far left, clockwise: smoked trout, oysters on the half shell, clams on the half*

d shrimp, spicy cocktail sauce, mignonette sauce, horseradish cream, scallop seviche, and stone crab claws

Facing page: Christmas party fare. *From center bottom, clockwise:* curried shrimp, chopped hard-cooked egg yolk, toasted coconut, orange segments and sliced bananas, chopped hard-cooked egg white, mango chutney, chopped scallions, popadams, guava jelly, and boiled rice

German Christmas dinner. *From far left, clockwise:* brussel sprouts, spaetzle, red cabbage, brown gravy, and roast goose with poached pears and Madeira-soaked prunes

Sautéed Snow Peas

YIELD: 8 TO 10 SERVINGS

3 pounds fresh snow peas
6 tablespoons unsalted
  butter, clarified
1 teaspoon salt
$\frac{1}{2}$ teaspoon freshly ground
  pepper

1. Soak the snow peas in cold water for 30 minutes. Drain the snow peas and trim the ends from the pods.

2. In a very large skillet, heat the clarified butter over high heat until it is quite hot. Add the pea pods to the skillet and cook them for 1 minute, stirring continuously with a metal spatula. Add the salt and pepper, and continue cooking and stirring for an additional minute. Transfer the peas to a warm serving dish and serve immediately.

Glazed Onions

YIELD: 8 TO 10 SERVINGS

24 small white onions,
  peeled
2 teaspoons salt
8 tablespoons unsalted
  butter (1 stick)
Freshly ground pepper to
  taste
1 tablespoon granulated
  sugar

1. Place the onions in a large saucepan, add enough water to cover and $1\frac{1}{2}$ teaspoons of the salt. Bring the water to a boil, reduce the heat, and simmer the onions, partially covered, for 12 to 14 minutes. Test for doneness with the point of a paring knife. They should still be a bit crisp. Drain the onions in a colander.

2. Heat the butter in a large heavy skillet, add the onions, and season them with the remaining $\frac{1}{2}$ teaspoon salt and the pepper. Sauté the onions over high heat, stirring them with a slotted spoon, until they start to color. Sprinkle the onions with the sugar and continue cooking and stirring until the sugar has glazed them and they are evenly browned. Transfer the onions to a serving dish.

◀ New Year's Eve favorites. *From lower right, clockwise: potted shrimp and toast, roast shell of beef and mushroom caps filled with a broccoli purée, French roast potatoes, sautéed cherry tomatoes with basil, trifle, and mixed green salad with vinaigrette*

Gratin Potatoes

2 cups milk
2 garlic cloves, crushed
8 tablespoons unsalted
  butter (1 stick)
3½ pounds boiling potatoes,
  peeled and cut into
  ⅛-inch-thick slices
1½ teaspoons salt
½ teaspoon freshly ground
  white pepper
1¾ cups grated Swiss
  cheese
¼ cup grated Parmesan
  cheese

1. Preheat the oven to 400°.

2. Place the milk and garlic in a saucepan, bring the milk to a boil, and set the pan aside.

3. Grease a 10-by-14-by-3½-inch ovenproof serving dish with 2 tablespoons of the butter.

4. Layer half of the potatoes in the dish, season with half of the salt and pepper, and scatter half of the grated Swiss cheese over the top. Layer the remaining potatoes in the dish, and sprinkle with the rest of the salt and pepper. Combine the remaining Swiss cheese with the Parmesan cheese and scatter the mixture evenly over the top of the potatoes. Dot the potatoes with the remaining butter.

5. Place an oven rack in the middle of the oven, pull it part way out, and place the baking dish on it. Pour the hot milk over the potatoes, remove the garlic cloves, and carefully slide the oven rack back in position.

6. Bake the potatoes for 30 minutes, or until all the milk is absorbed and the top is nicely browned. To test for doneness, pierce the potatoes with the tip of a paring knife.

Strawberry Cream Roll

Cake

2 tablespoons butter,
  softened
4 large egg whites
$\frac{1}{4}$ cup granulated sugar
4 large egg yolks
$\frac{1}{2}$ teaspoon vanilla extract
$\frac{1}{2}$ cup all-purpose flour

1. Preheat the oven to 400°.

2. Grease the inside of an 11-by-16-inch jelly-roll pan with 1 tablespoon of the butter. Line the pan with wax paper and coat the paper with the remaining tablespoon of butter.

3. Beat the egg whites until they hold soft peaks. Gradually add the sugar, and continue to beat until the whites are stiff.

4. Beat the yolks with a fork to break them up. Stir a large spoonful of the egg whites into the yolks, then pour the egg-yolk mixture over the remaining egg whites. Add the vanilla and, with a large rubber spatula, fold the mixture together, sifting in the flour $\frac{1}{4}$ cup at a time as you fold.

5. Pour the cake batter into the jelly-roll pan and spread it evenly with the spatula. Bake on a rack in the middle of the oven for 12 to 14 minutes, or until the cake is light gold in color and shrinks slightly from the sides of the pan.

Filling

1 pint fresh strawberries,
  washed and hulled
2 tablespoons imported
  kirsch
1$\frac{1}{2}$ cups heavy cream,
  chilled
$\frac{1}{2}$ teaspoon vanilla extract
8 tablespoons
  confectioners' sugar

1. Slice the strawberries and place them in a bowl. Sprinkle the berries with the kirsch and let them sit for 15 minutes.

2. Beat the heavy cream at moderate speed until it thickens slightly. Add the vanilla and 4 tablespoons of the confectioners' sugar, and continue to beat until the cream is of spreading consistency. Fold in the sliced berries and refrigerate the filling until the cake cools to room temperature.

3. Spread the cream mixture evenly over the top of the cake, then roll up the cake lengthwise jelly-roll fashion. Refrigerate. Just before serving, sift the remaining confectioners' sugar over the top of the cake.

```
┌─────────────────────────────────────┐
│  ┌───────────────────────────────┐  │
│  │           MENU                │  │
│  │  Mushroom-filled Puff Pastry  │  │
│  │       Lobster Newburg         │  │
│  │         Rice Pilaf            │  │
│  │       Green Bean Salad        │  │
│  │      Lemon Meringue Pie       │  │
│  └───────────────────────────────┘  │
└─────────────────────────────────────┘
```

Mushroom-filled Puff Pastry

YIELD: 10 TO 12 SERVINGS

3 tablespoons unsalted butter
2 tablespoons finely chopped shallots
1 pound mushrooms, thinly sliced
¼ cup flour
1 cup hot milk
1 cup hot heavy cream
1 teaspoon salt
½ teaspoon freshly ground pepper
2 tablespoons chopped flat-leaf parsley
12 ounces puff pastry or puff pastry scraps
1 or 2 eggs, beaten

1. Melt the butter over medium heat in a heavy saucepan. Add the shallots and cook until translucent. Add the mushrooms, cover the pan, and cook for 10 minutes. Remove the cover and cook over high heat to evaporate the liquid.

2. Lower the heat and, with a wooden spoon, stir in the flour and cook for a few minutes. Mix the milk and cream together and, with a wire whisk, gradually beat them into the flour mixture. Add the salt and pepper, and bring the mixture to the boil. Reduce the heat and simmer for 5 minutes.

3. Stir in the parsley, and scrape the mixture into a shallow dish. Chill until the mushroom filling is firm.

4. Roll the pastry into a 9-by-15-inch rectangle. Cut the rectangle in half lengthwise, and spread the chilled mushroom mixture down the center of one strip, leaving a 1-inch border all around the filling. Brush the border with the beaten egg. Cover with the remaining strip of pastry, securing the pastry edges together. Brush the entire top of the pastry with beaten egg. Place the pastry on a baking sheet and refrigerate for 30 minutes.

5. Preheat the oven to 400°.

6. Remove the pastry from the refrigerator and brush it again with beaten egg. Make two $\frac{1}{2}$-inch slits in the top of the pastry by piercing it with a small, sharp knife, then place it on a rack in the middle of the oven, and bake for 40 minutes, or until it has puffed and is deep brown in color. Let the pastry cool on a rack for a few minutes before slicing.

Note:

If you are using fresh puff pastry, before filling it prick the pastry all over with a fork.

Lobster Newburg

Unlike the original recipe for lobster Newburg, this one has a roux that stabilizes the egg yolks and keeps the sauce from curdling when it is served from a chafing dish.

YIELD: 10 TO 12 SERVINGS

8 tablespoons unsalted butter (1 stick)
1 tablespoon sweet imported paprika
$\frac{1}{2}$ cup all-purpose flour
5 cups fish stock, or fresh or canned chicken broth
1 cup heavy cream
$\frac{1}{2}$ cup dry sherry
5 pounds cooked lobster meat, cut into 1-inch chunks
4 egg yolks
Salt and pepper to taste

1. To make the sauce, melt the butter in a large saucepan over low heat. Add the paprika and stir until the paprika dissolves. Gradually add the flour, stirring with a wooden spoon until the mixture is smooth, and cook for 4 to 5 minutes. Remove the saucepan from the heat, and slowly add the stock or broth and the cream, beating the liquids into the flour mixture with a wire whisk. Return the saucepan to the heat, and bring the sauce to a boil to thicken. Lower the heat and let the sauce simmer for 20 minutes.

2. Add the sherry and lobster meat to the sauce. Beat the egg yolks together with $\frac{1}{2}$ cup of the hot sauce, then whisk the yolk mixture into the sauce in the saucepan and let the mixture cook 2 minutes longer. Do not let it come close to a boil or it might curdle. Add salt and pepper to taste.

Rice Pilaf

YIELD: 10 TO 12 SERVINGS

4 tablespoons butter
½ cup finely chopped onion
2 cups long-grain rice
4 cups chicken broth, fresh
  or canned
⅓ cup unsalted pistachio or
  pine nuts
Freshly ground pepper to
  taste
2 tablespoons finely
  chopped parsley

1. Heat the butter in a 3- to 4-quart casserole, add the onion, and cook until it is lightly browned. Add the rice and stir until the grains are evenly coated with the butter.

2. Pour in the chicken broth and bring it to a boil. Reduce the heat as low as possible, cover the casserole, and steam the rice for about 20 minutes, or until all the liquid has been absorbed. Remove the pan from the heat and let the rice stand, still covered, for 10 minutes before serving.

3. Just before serving, using a fork, stir in the nuts, freshly ground pepper, and chopped parsley.

Green Bean Salad

This salad is best made six to eight hours before serving. Wash the beans in the pot you will use for cooking them; it will help you to judge how much water is needed.

YIELD: 10 TO 12 SERVINGS

2 pounds green beans
Salt
Vinaigrette dressing (page
  79)
2 large onions, thinly sliced
1 teaspoon dried basil
2 large tomatoes, peeled,
  seeded, and coarsely
  chopped (optional)

1. Snap the ends of the beans off and wash the beans in cold running water.

2. Bring enough lightly salted water to cover the beans to a rolling boil, then add the beans and cook for 12 to 15 minutes, depending on the size of the beans. Taste them after 10 minutes; when done, they should still be a little crisp.

3. Drain the beans in a colander, then transfer them to a large bowl and, while they are still hot, mix them with the vinaigrette, thinly sliced onions, and basil. Turn the beans several times as they cool to room temperature. Add the tomatoes, if using them, cover with plastic wrap, and refrigerate. Remove the beans from the refrigerator several hours before serving.

Lemon Meringue Pie

Every day my good friend and talented pastry chef, Russell Carr, makes dozens of giant lemon meringue tartlets for my restaurant using the following recipe. (If you prefer individual servings, this recipe will yield four $4\frac{1}{2}$-inch tartlets.) The dessert is so popular that many people often call in advance to reserve it.

Pastry

YIELD: 6 TO 8 SERVINGS

$1\frac{1}{2}$ cups all-purpose flour
6 tablespoons unsalted
    butter, chilled and cut
    into small pieces
2 tablespoons vegetable
    shortening
2 teaspoons granulated
    sugar
$\frac{1}{4}$ teaspoon salt
3 to 5 tablespoons ice
    water

1. Place the flour, butter, shortening, sugar, and salt in a medium-sized bowl. With the tips of your fingers, rub the ingredients together until they form small granules. Sprinkle 3 tablespoons of the ice water over the pastry mixture and gather it into a ball. If the dough crumbles, add additional ice water, 1 tablespoon at a time; use only as much as it takes to shape the pastry into a ball. Press the dough into a thick cake, wrap it in wax paper, and refrigerate for 30 minutes.

2. Roll out the pastry into a 12-inch circle. Starting at one edge, roll the pastry onto the rolling pin. Lift the rolling pin, hold it over the pie pan so that about $1\frac{1}{2}$ inches of the pastry drops over the closest edge of the pan, then unroll the rest of the pastry, letting it fall into the pan. Gently fit the pastry into the pan and trim off the excess. Refrigerate for 1 hour to let the dough rest before baking.

3. Preheat the oven to 375°.

4. Fit a piece of heavy duty foil on top of the pastry. Place the pan on a rack in the middle of the oven and bake the pastry shell for 10 minutes. Remove the foil and prick the bottom of the pastry shell several times with the tines of a fork. Continue to bake the pastry shell for an additional 10 to 12 minutes, or until it is golden brown. Remove the pastry from the oven and let it cool to room temperature on a wire rack.

Filling

½ cup granulated sugar
⅓ cup cornstarch
Pinch salt
3 large egg yolks
1¾ cups milk
2 tablespoons butter
1 tablespoon finely grated
   lemon rind
⅓ cup lemon juice
6 tablespoons granulated
   sugar
1 tablespoon cornstarch
3 large egg whites

1. In a heavy saucepan (not aluminum), combine the sugar, cornstarch, and salt. Beat in the egg yolks and continue beating until the mixture forms a smooth yellow paste. Gradually whisk in the milk.

2. Whisking constantly, bring the mixture to a boil over medium heat. Remove from the heat and immediately beat in the butter, lemon rind, and lemon juice. Pour the mixture into the cooled pastry shell.

3. Preheat the oven to 400°.

4. When the filling has cooled to room temperature, make the meringue. Sift the sugar with the cornstarch. Beat the egg whites until they form soft peaks. Gradually add the sugar and continue to beat until the whites form stiff peaks.

5. Mound the meringue on top of the pie, or, if you wish, make decorations by piping the meringue through a pastry bag fitted with a number 5 star tube. Sift the confectioners' sugar over the top of the pie, place the pie on a rack in the middle of the oven, and bake for 10 minutes, or until the meringue is nicely browned.

Christmas Day Breakfast

The following breakfast menu is both extra-special and substantial, a good meal to serve if you are traveling any distance to visit on Christmas morning. It also makes a satisfying second or late breakfast after all the presents have been opened, when the grownups might like to toast the day with mimosas.

Eating the hash with a raw egg yolk is the way I enjoy it most. As you toss the yolk with the hot hash, it cooks slightly, making a delicious coating on the little cubes of meat and potatoes. I also add a few more grindings of fresh pepper. If you prefer, you can serve the hash with fried or poached eggs instead.

If your household is expanded by overnight guests, you may want to serve shirred eggs, the easiest way I know to cook eggs for a crowd. Simply butter small shallow ovenproof dishes and add an egg to each. Dribble a little melted butter over the eggs and bake them in the oven for six to eight minutes, or until they are set. They can be garnished with thin strips of ham, crumbled bacon, or a dollop of red caviar.

Some welcome additions to a hearty Christmas breakfast might be pancakes, good country sausages, broiled Irish slab bacon, a nice thick ham steak, or even the crisp potato pancakes on pages 83–84. Whatever breakfast you choose, it would not be complete without homemade brioche and stollen, topped with sweet butter and served with plenty of freshly brewed coffee or tea.

```
┌─────────────────────────────────────┐
│             MENU                     │
│        Broiled Grapefruit            │
│         Swedish Hash                 │
│        Brioche (page 28)             │
│       Stollen (pages 44–45)          │
│        Mimosa (page 69)              │
└─────────────────────────────────────┘
```

Broiled Grapefruit

YIELD: 4 SERVINGS

2 grapefruits
2 tablespoons honey
2 tablespoons unsalted
  butter, softened
4 teaspoons kirsch

1. Cut the grapefruits in half and, with a small serrated knife, loosen the sections from the membranes and the inner white skin.

2. Preheat the broiler.

3. Place the grapefruit halves in a shallow heatproof dish. Warm the butter and honey together in a saucepan until the butter melts. Remove the pan from the heat and stir in the kirsch. Spoon the mixture over the grapefruit halves, dividing it evenly between them.

4. Broil the grapefruit until the honey mixture bubbles, and serve.

Swedish Hash

4 tablespoons butter

2 tablespoons vegetable oil

6 small baking potatoes, cut into small dice

1 cup onions, finely chopped

1 pound leftover roast beef or lamb, cut into small dice

8 ounces ham, cut into small dice

Freshly ground pepper to taste

2 tablespoons chopped parsley

4 egg yolks, each in a half shell

1. In a large skillet, heat 2 tablespoons of the butter with the vegetable oil until they are very hot. Add the potatoes and fry them, stirring and turning them with a metal spatula until they are golden brown. Remove the potatoes from the skillet and set them on paper towels to drain.

2. Heat the remaining 2 tablespoons butter in the same skillet, add the onions, and cook them until soft and translucent. Add the diced meats and cook a few minutes until just heated through. Return the cooked potatoes to the skillet and toss all the ingredients together, adding a few grindings of freshly ground pepper and the chopped parsley. Transfer the hash to a heated serving platter and serve with the egg yolks; set the egg-yolk-filled half shells next to the hash, or push them lightly into the top of the hash. (See the second color section.)

Traditional Dinners

The keeping of Christmas traditions seems to increase the pleasure of the holidays. However, when it comes to cooking, don't feel that you can't make a few alterations in traditional menus. Certain of the dishes in the following menus are very acceptably interchangeable. The purée of celery root may be served with the roast turkey; the turnips and Brussels sprouts go well with the roast beef; and to accompany the goose, mashed potatoes can replace the spaetzle and plum pudding can be served instead of wine jelly.

So that you as well as your guests can enjoy Christmas dinner, here are some suggestions for budgeting your time. For the English dinner, the pickled shrimp may be made several days early. The hard sauce for the plum pudding (made weeks before) can also be made several days ahead. The batter for the Yorkshire pudding can be made the day before. For the American dinner, make the stuffing weeks ahead and freeze it. Prepare the cranberry sauce and relish several days ahead. Early Christmas morning, peel the potatoes and turnips and keep them in cold water. Also in the morning, bake the mincemeat tartlets. For the German dinner, the consommé with marrow balls can be made and frozen a month before. The pears and prunes as well as the red cabbage can be made several days ahead. In fact, reheating improves the red cabbage; if it loses its color add a tablespoon of vinegar while it heats. The wine jelly can be made three or four days in advance. You can even cook the spaetzle two days ahead, then fry it in butter just before serving. It's wonderful this way.

ENGLISH MENU

Pickled Shrimp (page 62)

Standing Rib Roast of Beef

Yorkshire Pudding

Purée of Celery Root and Potatoes

Plum Pudding (pages 10–11)

Standing Rib Roast of Beef

YIELD: 8 TO 10 SERVINGS

*3-rib (8- to 10-pound)
   standing roast of beef*
$\frac{1}{4}$ *cup coarse salt*
*1$\frac{1}{2}$ teaspoons freshly
   ground pepper*

1. Preheat the oven to 500°.

2. Place the rib roast in a large shallow roasting pan, fat side up. Mix the salt and pepper together in a small bowl and spread it over the fat.

3. Place the roasting pan on a rack in the lower part of the oven and roast the beef for 20 minutes. Reduce the heat to 350° and continue to roast the meat: allow 18 minutes per pound (140° on a meat thermometer) for rare, 22 minutes per pound (or 160°) for medium, and 25 minutes per pound (or 170°) for well done.

4. Transfer the roast to a heated platter and let it rest for 20 to 30 minutes before carving.

Yorkshire Pudding

Instead of baking the pudding in a roasting pan as the recipe suggests, I very often bake it in a 1½-quart soufflé dish, and it comes out of the oven looking like a giant popover.

YIELD: 8 TO 10 SERVINGS

3 large eggs
¾ teaspoon salt
1½ cups all-purpose flour
1¼ cups milk
¼ cup roast beef drippings

1. In a large mixing bowl, beat the eggs with the salt. Gradually add the flour and continue beating until the mixture forms a yellow paste. Pour in the milk in a thin stream, stirring constantly. Strain the batter through a fine sieve and refrigerate for at least 1 hour.

2. Preheat the oven to 400°.

3. Place the roasting pan with ¼ cup of the beef drippings on a rack in the middle of the oven. When the fat is very hot, remove the batter from the refrigerator, stir it a few times, and pour it into the roasting pan. Bake the Yorkshire pudding for 15 minutes, then reduce the heat to 350° and continue to bake the pudding until it has risen and is crisp and brown, about 15 minutes longer.

4. Remove the pudding from the oven and immediately cut it into 4-inch-square portions. Serve with the standing rib roast or with the shell roast of beef on page 133.

Purée of Celery Root and Potatoes

YIELD: 8 TO 10 SERVINGS

1½ to 2 pounds celery root, peeled and cut into ¼-inch-thick slices
1 to 1½ pounds boiling potatoes, peeled and sliced in half
6 tablespoons unsalted butter, softened
¾ cup hot milk
1 teaspoon salt
¼ teaspoon freshly ground pepper

1. Boil the celery root in lightly salted water for 30 minutes. Add the potatoes and continue to boil, partially covered, for an additional 20 minutes or until both vegetables are cooked through. Test them for doneness with the tip of a paring knife. Drain the vegetables in a colander.

2. Melt the butter in the milk and keep the mixture warm.

3. Put the vegetables through a ricer or food mill. Beat in the butter and milk mixture and season with the salt and pepper.

AMERICAN MENU

Oysters with Mignonette Sauce (page 62)

Roast Turkey with Sausage Stuffing

Cranberry Sauce and/or
Cranberry-Orange-Nut Relish

Mashed Potatoes

Mashed Yellow Turnips

Broccoli Florets

Mincemeat Tartlets (pages 34–35)

Roast Turkey with Sausage Stuffing

Roasting a turkey on a rack in a shallow roasting pan allows the dry heat of the oven to circulate around the bird. In a deep roasting pan moisture will be created around the bird, which will prevent its browning well. By turning the bird four times while it is roasting, the skin becomes crisp and evenly golden in color.

Stuffing

YIELD: 8 TO 10 SERVINGS

8 cups dry bread cubes
12 tablespoons butter (1½ sticks)
1½ cups finely chopped celery
2 cups finely chopped onions
1 pound sausage meat
¼ cup parsley
2 teaspoons dried sage
1 egg, beaten
Salt and pepper to taste

1. Place the bread cubes in a large bowl and set aside.

2. Heat the butter in a large skillet. Add the celery and cook for 3 or 4 minutes, then add the onion and cook until both are soft and translucent. Scrape the mixture into the bowl with the bread cubes.

3. Set the skillet over low heat, add the sausage meat, and break the meat up as it cooks. When the meat turns light brown, transfer it with a slotted spoon to the bowl.

4. When the sausage meat is cool enough to handle, add the chopped parsley, dried sage, and beaten egg. With your hands, mix the ingredients thoroughly. Add salt and pepper to taste.

Turkey

One 12-pound turkey
4 tablespoons butter (½ stick)

1. Preheat the oven to 425°.

2. Pat the turkey dry with paper towels. Stuff the breast and large cavity with the stuffing. Close the openings by securing them with small metal skewers. Truss the turkey with butcher cord and place it on its side on a rack in a large shallow roasting pan. Spread the 4 tablespoons of butter over the turkey skin.

3. Roast the turkey on a rack in the lower middle area of the oven for 15 minutes. Turn the bird on its other side and roast it for an additional 15 minutes. Turn the turkey, breast side down, lower the heat to 350° and roast for 1 hour longer, basting the bird occasionally with the drippings. Turn the turkey breast side up and roast for 1 more hour, basting intermittently. Test for doneness by piercing the thigh with the tip of a paring knife; if the juice runs clear, the turkey is done. Transfer the turkey to a warm serving platter and remove the trussing cord. Let the turkey sit for 15 to 20 minutes before carving.

Gravy

Turkey neck and innards
1 small carrot, coarsely chopped
1 onion, coarsely chopped
2 large sprigs of parsley
1 bay leaf
2 cups water
2 cups chicken broth, fresh or canned
6 tablespoons flour

1. To make stock for the gravy, with a cleaver, chop the turkey neck into 1-inch pieces and combine in a pot with all the remaining ingredients, except the flour. Bring to a boil over high heat. Reduce the heat to low and simmer, partially covered, for 1½ hours.

2. Strain the stock and discard the solids.

3. Skim off all but about 3 tablespoons of fat from the roasting pan used for the turkey. Stir in the flour and cook for about 2 minutes. Pour in 2 cups of the strained stock (save the remaining stock for another use) and, with a metal spatula, scrape all the brown bits from the bottom and sides of the pan. When the gravy comes to a boil, reduce the heat, and let it simmer for 5 minutes.

4. Strain the gravy into a saucepan and keep it warm over very low heat for several minutes until you are ready to serve the turkey.

Cranberry Sauce or Cranberry-Orange-Nut Relish

No cranberry sauce is as good as the homemade variety, which is easy to make and can be prepared several days in advance. Here are two very different recipes that I sometimes serve together by filling center of the molded cranberry sauce with the relish.

Cranberry Sauce

YIELD: 8 TO 10 SERVINGS

2 cups water
2 cups granulated sugar
4 cups fresh cranberries
1 tablespoon grated orange rind

1. Combine the water and sugar in a medium-sized saucepan and stir over low heat until the sugar dissolves. Bring the syrup to a boil and add the cranberries. Boil the berries until the skins pop; this will take about 5 minutes. Stir in the orange rind and pour the mixture into a wet 4- to 6-cup ring mold. Chill in the refrigerator for several hours, or until firm enough to unmold.

2. To unmold the cranberry sauce, dip the mold into hot water for just a few seconds and dry with paper towels. Invert a well-chilled serving plate over the top of the mold and, with both hands holding the plate and the mold tightly together, turn them over, and remove the mold.

Cranberry-Orange-Nut Relish

YIELD: ABOUT 1 PINT

1 large orange
2 cups fresh cranberries
1 cup granulated sugar
½ cup coarsely chopped walnuts

1. Wash the orange, cut it into eighths, and remove any seeds.

2. Place the orange, cranberries, and granulated sugar in the container of a food processor and process the ingredients by turning the machine on and off quickly until the mixture becomes coarse pulp. Scrape the mixture into a bowl and stir in the chopped walnuts. Refrigerate for at least 2 hours before serving.

Mashed Potatoes

To keep mashed potatoes warm when serving a large group of people, place a trivet on the bottom of a large pot that is one-third full of hot water. Place the container of mashed potatoes on the trivet and cover the potatoes with a piece of buttered wax paper, buttered side down. Cover the pot with a lid and set it over a very low flame. In this fashion you can keep the potatoes hot for an hour or longer.

YIELD: 8 TO 10 SERVINGS

5 pounds boiling potatoes
4 teaspoons salt
8 tablespoons butter (1 stick)
1 cup milk, approximately
½ teaspoon ground white pepper

1. Peel and wash the potatoes, place them in a large pot and cover them with cold water. Add 3 teaspoons of the salt, bring the water to a boil, and cook with the pot partially covered for about 20 minutes. Test the potatoes for doneness with the tip of a paring knife.

2. Drain the potatoes in a colander. Return the potatoes to the pot and mash with a potato masher, or mash in an electric mixer.

3. Combine the butter and 1 cup of milk in a small saucepan and heat the mixture until the butter is melted and the milk is hot. Gradually beat the milk mixture into the potato purée; if it is too dry, add a little additional milk. Beat in the remaining 1 teaspoon of salt and the pepper.

Mashed Yellow Turnips

Mashed rutabagas, which we called yellow turnips, always found their way onto my mother's holiday table, and they were always appreciated, even by people who thought they didn't like the vegetable. Her secret, learned from her German mother, was a touch of sugar, which made all the difference. If you have any leftovers, try combining the turnips with mashed potatoes in equal proportions. It's a delicious variation for both vegetables.

YIELD: 8 TO 10 SERVINGS

3 pounds yellow turnips, or rutabagas
½ teaspoon granulated sugar
½ teaspoon salt
¼ teaspoon pepper
6 tablespoons unsalted butter

1. Peel the turnips and cut them into large cubes. Wash the cubes, place them in a large saucepan, and cover with salted water. Bring the water to a boil over high heat and cook the turnips for about 15 minutes, or until tender.

2. Drain the turnips in a colander, return them to the saucepan, and mash with a potato masher. Add the sugar, salt, pepper, and butter.

Broccoli Florets or Green Beans

With the richness of the sausage stuffing and giblet gravy and the textures of both the mashed potatoes and turnips, this menu would not be complete without the crispness and color of a simply and perfectly cooked green vegetable, for example, broccoli florets or green beans.

Broccoli Florets

YIELD: 8 TO 10 SERVINGS

3 pounds broccoli
6 tablespoons unsalted
butter, melted
Salt and pepper to taste

1. Trim off and discard the thick stems of the broccoli stalks and separate the tops into florets. Wash the broccoli in cold running water.

2. In a large saucepan, bring enough lightly salted water to cover the broccoli to a rolling boil, drop in the broccoli, and cook for 8 to 10 minutes. Test the broccoli by piercing the stems with the tip of a paring knife. It should be slightly firm.

3. Drain the broccoli in a colander, then transfer it to a large, warmed bowl. Toss it with the melted butter, and season to taste with the salt and pepper.

Green Beans

YIELD: 8 TO 10 SERVINGS

2 pounds green beans
4 tablespoons unsalted
butter, melted
Salt and pepper to taste

1. Snap off the ends of the beans and wash the beans in cold running water.

2. In a large saucepan, bring enough lightly salted water to cover the beans to a rolling boil. Drop in the beans and cook for 12 to 15 minutes, depending on the size of the beans. After 10 minutes, test the beans for doneness; when done, they should still be a little crisp.

3. Drain the beans in a colander, then transfer them to a large, warmed bowl. Toss them with the melted butter, and season to taste with salt and pepper.

Roast Ducks with Quince

More often than not our Thanksgiving dinner is repeated on Christmas day. If you have had your fill of turkey, I suggest you replace it with roast ducks with quince, and serve the meal with the same choice of vegetables.

Quince

YIELD: 6 TO 8 SERVINGS

1 large quince, peeled,
   quartered, and cored
$\frac{1}{4}$ cup fresh lemon juice

The day or morning before serving, place the quince pieces in a medium-sized saucepan, cover with cold water and add the lemon juice. Bring the water to a boil, reduce the heat, and simmer the quince partially covered for 45 minutes, or until the pieces can easily be pierced with the tip of a paring knife. Drain the quince, place the pieces in a small bowl, cover with plastic wrap, and store in the refrigerator.

Sauce

The necks and second wing
   sections of the ducks
2 tablespoons butter
1 cup chopped onions
$\frac{1}{4}$ cup diced carrot
$\frac{1}{2}$ cup diced celery
$\frac{1}{2}$ teaspoon thyme
1 cup dry red wine
2 cups chicken broth, fresh
   or canned
$\frac{1}{4}$ cup currant jelly
2 tablespoons arrowroot
1 tablespoon water

1. The day or morning before serving, chop the necks and wing sections of the ducks into 1-inch pieces with a cleaver.

2. Melt the butter in a large heavy skillet, and when it is hot, add the chopped pieces of duck, and brown them evenly on all sides. Stir in the chopped onion, carrot, and celery and let them cook until they brown lightly. Add the thyme, then the red wine, and reduce the wine to $\frac{1}{2}$ cup. Pour in the chicken broth and bring the liquid to a boil. Reduce the heat and let the stock simmer partially covered for $1\frac{1}{2}$ hours.

3. Remove the skillet from the heat and strain the stock through a sieve into a heatproof bowl. Press down on the solids with the back of a wooden spoon to get all the juices, then discard the solids remaining in the sieve.

4. Return the stock to the skillet, stir in the currant jelly and let it melt. Mix the arrowroot and water together and stir them into the sauce. Cook for a few minutes, or until the sauce thickens slightly. Pour the sauce into a storage container and, when it cools to room temperature, cover it with plastic wrap and store it in the refrigerator.

Ducks

Two 5- to 6-pound ducks
1 teaspoon salt
½ teaspoon freshly ground
  pepper
1 teaspoon thyme
2 medium-sized onions,
  peeled
2 large garlic cloves,
  crushed

1. The day before cooking, pat the ducks dry with paper towels. Cut off the second section of each wing and reserve the sections for the sauce. Pull out and discard all the fat from the cavity ends of each duck. Stuff the ducks with paper towels, then wrap them in several layers of paper towels and refrigerate overnight. (The towels absorb a lot of moisture from the ducks, which helps to make them cook more evenly crisp and brown.)

2. Preheat the oven to 450°.

3. Unwrap the ducks and remove the paper towels from the cavities. Season the cavities with the salt, pepper, and thyme. Place 1 onion and 1 crushed garlic clove into the cavity of each bird.

4. Place the ducks, breast side up and slightly apart, on a rack in a large shallow roasting pan. Set the pan on a rack in the middle of the oven, and roast the ducks for 30 minutes.

5. Remove the pan from the oven and pour off the fat into a heatproof disposable container. Turn the ducks breast side down and return them to the oven. Reduce the heat to 350°, and continue to roast the ducks 30 minutes longer.

6. Drain off the fat and turn the ducks breast side up again. Roast the ducks an additional 30 minutes.

7. Remove the quince and sauce from the refrigerator. Cut the quince into medium-sized dice and set aside.

8. Transfer the ducks to a warm serving platter and keep them warm in a low oven with the door open. Pour off all the fat from the roasting pan. Add the sauce to the pan and place the pan over medium heat. With a metal spatula scrape all the brown bits from the bottom and sides of the pan. Add the quince and pour the sauce into a saucepan and keep warm over low heat.

9. To serve, quarter the ducks and spoon some of the sauce over them. Serve the remaining sauce in a heated sauceboat.

```
┌─────────────────────────────────────────┐
│                                         │
│          GERMAN MENU                    │
│   Consommé with Marrow Balls            │
│  Roast Goose with Pears and Prunes      │
│          Red Cabbage                    │
│           Spaetzle                      │
│   Brussels Sprouts with Chestnuts       │
│          Wine Jelly                     │
│                                         │
└─────────────────────────────────────────┘
```

Consommé with Marrow Balls

A consommé made with a well-flavored beef stock, and with the addition of marrow balls, a typical German touch, makes a delicious, light starter for the roast goose dinner that follows. The optional ground beef called for in the recipe not only helps to clarify the stock but also turns the stock into a double consommé that can be garnished in countless different ways.

To make the broth for the consommé, follow the vegetable-beef soup recipe on page 145 through step 2. Let the broth cool to room temperature, or chill it overnight in the refrigerator.

Consommé

YIELD: 6 TO 8 SERVINGS

½ cup chopped celery
  leaves
½ cup chopped onions
½ cup chopped carrots
¼ cup chopped parsley
  stems
2 large tomatoes, coarsely
  chopped
4 egg whites
4 egg shells, crushed
1 pound very lean ground
  beef (optional)
Pepper and salt to taste
12 cups beef broth, page 145

1. Place all the consommé ingredients in a large bowl and, with your hands, combine them thoroughly. Add them to the beef broth and bring to a boil over high heat. Reduce the heat and simmer the broth for 30 minutes.

2. In the meantime, line a large sieve with a double thickness of wet cheesecloth and place it over a large pot or heatproof bowl. When the consommé is ready, pour it into the sieve and let the liquid drain through. Discard the ingredients in the sieve and taste the consommé for seasoning. Reheat, and add the marrow balls before serving.

Marrow Balls

⅓ cup fresh marrow, melted
¼ teaspoon salt
Pinch nutmeg
3 egg yolks
1 tablespoon chopped
   parsley
¾ cup packaged cracker
   crumbs, approximately

1. To make the marrow balls, combine the marrow, salt, nutmeg, egg yolks, and parsley. Add the cracker crumbs gradually, stirring the mixture with a fork until it thickens enough to be shaped. With your hands, form small balls about 1 inch in diameter and refrigerate them for 1 hour.

2. Cook the marrow balls in simmering and lightly salted water for 12 to 14 minutes, or until they rise to the surface. With a slotted spoon, transfer the marrow balls to a tray lined with paper towels if you need to hold them for a while, or place them directly in the hot consommé for serving.

Roast Goose with Pears and Prunes

Because goose is so fatty, it tends to make any stuffing quite greasy. Therefore, instead of a stuffing, I always prefer to serve accompaniments that will fully complement the goose's rich flavor. Poached pears and prunes are some of my favorites, and they can be prepared several days in advance and stored covered in the refrigerator. Remove them several hours before serving, however. To add more color around the goose, fill in around the fruit with some sprigs of parsley or watercress. If time and refrigerator space are at a premium, you can always resort to canned pear halves packed in natural juices. And, if you like, you can omit the prunes and place a teaspoon or so of red currant jelly into the cavity of each pear.

Goose

YIELD: 6 TO 8 SERVINGS

One 8- to 10-pound goose
Salt
Pepper
3 large onions, quartered
2 large garlic cloves,
   crushed

1. Preheat the oven to 325°.

2. Pull out all the fat from the inside of the goose and pat the goose dry, inside and out, with paper towels. Season the breast cavity with salt and pepper, and stuff it with the onions and garlic.

3. Set the goose, breast side up, on a rack in a large, shallow roasting pan. Cook on a rack in the middle of the oven for 2 hours and 45 minutes. Every 20 minutes or so, remove the fat from the bottom of the pan with a large metal kitchen spoon or bulb baster. To test for doneness, punc-

ture a thigh with the point of a knife; when the juice runs pale yellow, the goose is done.

4. Transfer the goose to a warm serving platter. Let it rest for 15 minutes, and then serve it garnished with the pears and prunes. To make gravy, follow the instructions for the roast turkey gravy, page 119.

Poached Pears

4 cups water
½ cup granulated sugar
1 tablespoon lemon juice
4 pears

1. Combine the water, sugar, and lemon juice in a large shallow pan.

2. Peel each pear and cut it in half lengthwise. Scoop out the core with a melon baller, and place the pear halves in the water mixture.

3. Bring the liquid to a boil, reduce the heat to a simmer, and cook the pears for 8 to 12 minutes. Test for doneness with the tip of a paring knife. The pears should remain slightly firm. Transfer the pears and the liquid to a bowl, and let them cool to room temperature.

Prunes in Madeira

8 large pitted prunes
½ cup Madeira

1. Place the prunes in a small saucepan and cover them with cold water. Bring the water to a boil, remove the prunes from the heat, and let them sit for 1 hour.

2. Drain the prunes, place them in a small bowl, and pour the Madeira over them. Let the prunes macerate for at least 2 hours.

Red Cabbage

YIELD: 6 TO 8 SERVINGS

One 3-pound head of red cabbage
3 tablespoons butter
1 cup coarsely chopped onions
3 tart apples, peeled, cored, and coarsely chopped
$\frac{1}{4}$ cup red wine vinegar
1 tablespoon sugar
$1\frac{1}{2}$ teaspoons salt
1 bay leaf
4 cups water

1. Remove any bruised leaves from the cabbage and wash it under cold running water. Quarter the cabbage and remove and discard the core. Thinly shred the cabbage with a large knife.

2. Heat the butter until very hot in a large casserole. Add the chopped onions and cook them until lightly browned. Add the cabbage, apples, wine vinegar, sugar, salt, bay leaf, and water. Bring the liquid to a boil, reduce the heat to very low, and let the cabbage simmer, partially covered, for about 2 hours or until very soft. Check the casserole from time to time; if it seems dry, add an additional $\frac{1}{2}$ cup of water.

Spaetzle

YIELD: 6 TO 8 SERVINGS

10 tablespoons butter
4 slices white bread, crusts removed, processed into coarse, fresh bread crumbs
3 cups all-purpose flour
$\frac{1}{2}$ teaspoon salt
Pinch of ground nutmeg
3 eggs, lightly beaten
1 cup water

1. In a small sauté pan, heat 8 tablespoons of the butter until the butter is very hot. Add the bread crumbs and stir with a wooden spoon until they take on a deep golden color. Transfer the bread crumbs to a paper towel and set aside.

2. Combine the flour, salt, nutmeg, and the beaten eggs in a mixing bowl. Gradually add the water and, with a large spoon, stir the heavy batter until it is free of all lumps.

3. Bring 4 quarts of salted water to a boil in a large pot. Hold a colander with large holes over the pot and, with a wooden spoon, press $\frac{1}{3}$ of the batter at a time through the holes into the water. Stir the spaetzle with the spoon to keep them from sticking together and continue boiling them for 8 minutes, or until they are tender.

4. Drain the spaetzle in the colander. Melt the butter in the same pot over low heat, return the drained spaetzle to the pot, and toss them in the butter. Transfer to a serving dish and sprinkle with the toasted bread crumbs.

Brussels Sprouts with Chestnuts

YIELD: 6 TO 8 SERVINGS

*12 tablespoons unsalted
 butter (1½ sticks)*
6 cups Brussels sprouts
*2 cups canned chestnuts
 packed in water*
½ teaspoon salt
*Freshly ground black
 pepper to taste*
Pinch of sugar

1. Wash the Brussels sprouts and trim off any bad leaves.

2. Melt the butter in a large skillet (not cast iron or aluminum, which will give the sprouts a metallic flavor). Add the sprouts, salt, pepper, and sugar, and stir them with a spoon until they are well coated with butter. Cover the pan and simmer the sprouts over low heat for 10 minutes.

3. Chop the chestnuts coarsely and stir them into the sprouts, then cover and cook for an additional 5 minutes or until the sprouts are just crisply tender. Test for doneness with the tip of a paring knife. Serve in a warm dish.

Wine Jelly

Elizabeth Wright of Wilmington, North Carolina, served me this wine jelly—the first I have ever liked. It has a wonderful flavor, its clear, brilliant topaz color is exquisite, and it makes a light, refreshing dessert even when the center is heaped with whipped cream.

YIELD: 6 TO 8 SERVINGS

*3 packages unflavored
 gelatin*
3 cups dry sherry
¼ cup lemon juice
4 sticks cinnamon
Rind of one lemon
2½ cups granulated sugar
2½ cups water

1. Place the gelatin in a small heatproof bowl. Add ¾ cup of the sherry and the lemon juice. When the gelatin has softened, set the bowl in a skillet of simmering water until the gelatin dissolves. Remove the skillet from the heat and set it aside, leaving the bowl of gelatin in the hot water.

2. Boil the cinnamon and lemon rind in the 2½ cups of water for 10 minutes. Add the sugar, let it dissolve, and then add the gelatin and the remaining 2¼ cups of sherry.

3. Line a large strainer with a double thickness of wet cheesecloth and set it over a medium-sized pot or heatproof bowl. Strain the sherry mixture, then pour it into a wet 6-cup ring mold and refrigerate for several hours, or until set.

4. To unmold the wine jelly, dip the mold into hot water for just a few seconds and dry it with paper towels. Place a well-chilled inverted serving plate over the top of the mold and, with both hands holding the plate and the mold tightly together, turn them over and remove the mold.

New Year's Eve Buffet

Although both the menus below have been planned for a minimum of last-minute effort, they are not alike in style. In fact, I designed them with two very different types of party in mind. The roast shell of beef menu works beautifully for a formal sit-down buffet dinner. Preparations can be started two to three days ahead by making the cake and custard for the trifle. The day before the dinner, make the potted shrimp. Early on the day of the party, prepare the stuffed mushrooms for baking and blanch and peel the tomatoes. Peel the potatoes and keep them in cold water so that they don't discolor. Late in the afternoon, assemble the trifle and have the shell of beef in the roasting pan ready for the oven. If you follow these instructions, your dinner will be completely under control and you will have time to relax before the celebrating begins.

The roast fresh ham does well for a less formal dinner and, if you choose to serve the ham at room temperature, which many prefer, there won't be any last-minute preparation at all. You can make the potato salad two to three days ahead, remembering to taste for salt before serving it. Make the beet and onion salad at the same time. One-day-old coleslaw is even better than fresh, and the chocolate mousse can also be made a day ahead.

Preparing either of these menus will leave you with plenty of energy for ringing in the New Year, and they will also give you a head start on a New Year's resolution to be organized about your entertaining!

```
                 ┌─────────────────────────────────────────┐
                 │                                         │
                 │                 MENU                    │
                 │                                         │
                 │            Potted Shrimp                │
                 │                                         │
                 │          Shell Roast of Beef            │
                 │                                         │
                 │          French Roast Potatoes          │
                 │                                         │
                 │        Cherry Tomatoes with Basil       │
                 │                                         │
                 │     Mushroom Caps with Broccoli Purée   │
                 │                                         │
                 │          Mixed Green Salad with         │
                 │   Garlic-flavored Vinaigrette Dressing  │
                 │                                         │
                 │                 Trifle                  │
                 │                                         │
                 │           Chocolate Truffles            │
                 │                                         │
                 └─────────────────────────────────────────┘
```

Potted Shrimp

Potted shrimp are traditionally made with tiny shrimp, which count about 65 to a pound. These shrimp can only be purchased frozen, however, and I find them quite tasteless. Therefore, I use fresh or frozen shrimp from Florida, which I chop into small pieces and season lightly with mace. They make wonderful potted shrimp, especially when served on oast made from the homemade white bread on page 46.

YIELD: 8 TO 10 SERVINGS

¾ pound unsalted butter (3 sticks)
1½ pounds medium-sized shrimp
1½ teaspoons salt
1 teaspoon ground mace
¼ teaspoon ground nutmeg
A few drops of Tabasco sauce

1. Clarify 12 tablespoons of the butter by placing it in a small saucepan and melting it over low heat. With a small spoon, remove and discard all the foam from the melted butter, leaving the clear butter fat in the pan.

2. Peel and devein the shrimp. Remove and reserve ½ inch of the tail section of 8 to 10 shrimp for decoration, and chop the remaining shrimp into very small pieces.

3. Heat the remaining 12 tablespoons of butter in a large shallow saucepan. Add the salt, mace, nutmeg, Tabasco sauce, and chopped shrimp, and toss the shrimp in the butter until they just turn pink.

4. Spoon the shrimp mixture into eight to ten ¼-cup ca-

pacity ramekins and cover with a thin layer of the clarified butter. Place a reserved shrimp tail on top of each ramekin, and place the ramekins in the refrigerator for 1 hour.

5. Remove the ramekins from the refrigerator and brush each shrimp tail with additional clarified butter to keep it moist. Return the potted shrimp to the refrigerator for at least 4 hours before serving.

Shell Roast of Beef

This roast is quite expensive; however, there is very little waste because any trimmings make a wonderful soup or a hearty stew.

YIELD: 8 TO 10 SERVINGS

One 6-pound shell beef roast
$\frac{1}{4}$ cup coarse salt
$1\frac{1}{2}$ teaspoons freshly ground pepper

1. Preheat the oven to 350°.

2. Place the shell roast on a rack in a large shallow roasting pan. Mix the salt and pepper together in a small bowl and spread it over the top of the roast.

3. Place the roasting pan on the middle rack of the oven and roast the beef to the degree of doneness desired: for rare, 15 minutes per pound (140° on a meat thermometer); for medium, 18 minutes per pound (or 160°); and for well done, 22 minutes per pound (or 170°). Transfer the roast to a heated platter and let it rest for 10 to 15 minutes before slicing.

French Roast Potatoes

YIELD: 8 TO 10 SERVINGS

$\frac{3}{4}$ cup clarified butter (see potted shrimp on preceding page)
14 baking potatoes, uniform in size, peeled
Salt and pepper to taste

1. Preheat the oven to 375°.

2. Place the clarified butter in a large shallow roasting pan and roll the potatoes in the butter to coat them evenly. Place the pan on a rack in the middle of the oven and roast the potatoes for about 1 hour, turning them and basting them occasionally with the butter. The potatoes are done when they are golden brown and can be easily pierced with the point of a paring knife.

3. With a slotted spoon, transfer the potatoes to a warm serving dish. Season with salt and pepper.

Cherry Tomatoes with Basil

The time it takes to peel the cherry tomatoes is well spent because it changes their shiny, somewhat plastic appearance to a rich texture more like velvet. And nothing enhances the flavor of tomatoes like fresh basil.

<u>YIELD: 8 TO 10 SERVINGS</u>

3 pints cherry tomatoes
6 tablespoons unsalted
   butter
$\frac{1}{4}$ cup fresh basil, coarsely
   chopped
$\frac{1}{2}$ teaspoon salt
$\frac{1}{4}$ teaspoon freshly ground
   pepper

1. In a large saucepan, bring 4 quarts of water to a boil over high heat. Drop the tomatoes into the water and blanch them for about 10 seconds. Pour the tomatoes into a colander and run cold water over them for 2 or 3 minutes to stop them from cooking.

2. With a paring knife, peel each tomato. Set the tomatoes aside in a bowl.

3. Minutes before serving, heat the butter in a large shallow skillet. Add the tomatoes to the skillet and toss them with a slotted spoon. Season with the basil, salt and pepper.

Mushroom Caps with Broccoli Purée

<u>YIELD: 14 FILLED MUSHROOM CAPS</u>

14 large white mushroom
   caps
6 tablespoons unsalted
   butter, melted
$\frac{3}{4}$ pound cleaned and
   trimmed broccoli, cut
   into large pieces
1 medium-sized boiling
   potato, peeled and cut in
   half
$\frac{1}{2}$ teaspoon salt
$\frac{1}{4}$ teaspoon white pepper

1. Preheat the oven to 400°.

2. Wipe the mushroom caps clean with damp paper towels and place them stem side up, on a jelly-roll pan. Dribble 4 tablespoons of the butter over them and season them lightly with salt and pepper. Bake the mushroom caps in the oven for 10 minutes, remove them from the oven, and set aside to cool.

3. Cook the broccoli in lightly salted water for 10 to 12 minutes, or until tender. With a slotted spoon, remove the broccoli from the pan and set it in a colander to drain. Cook the potato in the same boiling water for 12 to 16 minutes, or until tender.

4. Place the broccoli and the potato in the container of a food processor, and purée them with the remaining 2 tablespoons of butter, the salt and pepper. Correct the seasoning as necessary.

5. Using a small spoon, mound the purée in the mushroom caps. If you wish to hold the mushrooms this way for several hours before serving, brush the purée with a little more melted butter and store the mushrooms in a cool place; do not refrigerate.

6. Preheat the oven to 400°.

7. Place the stuffed mushrooms on a rack in the middle of the oven and bake for 10 minutes.

Chocolate Truffles

Like the Christmas log, chocolate truffles are very popular in France at Christmas time. This deliciously rich chocolate confection is often served after dessert and with coffee. Since they can be made weeks in advance and frozen, the truffles are also practical to make as gifts.

YIELD: ABOUT 36 TRUFFLES

16 ounces semisweet
   chocolate
$1\frac{3}{4}$ cups heavy cream
3 tablespoons Grand
   Marnier
$\frac{1}{2}$ cup unsweetened cocoa

1. With a large knife, chop the chocolate into small pieces, and place them in a large bowl.

2. Bring the cream to a boil and pour it over the chopped chocolate. With a wooden spoon, stir the chocolate and cream together until the chocolate has completely melted. Add the Grand Marnier.

3. Pour the mixture into a jelly-roll pan, and place the pan in the refrigerator until the chocolate hardens; this will take about 1 hour.

4. Shape the chocolate into small balls slightly less than 1 inch in diameter, place them on a jelly-roll pan, and refrigerate.

5. Before serving, sift the cocoa over the truffles and gently shake the jelly-roll pan back and forth so that the truffles will be completely covered with the cocoa. To serve, place the truffles in tiny foil candy cups.

Trifle

This festive-looking dessert is particularly easy to serve to large groups of people. Both the cake and the custard can be prepared several days in advance.

Cake

YIELD: 8 TO 10 SERVINGS

1½ cups all-purpose flour
9 large eggs
1½ cups granulated sugar
¾ teaspoon vanilla extract
8 tablespoons butter,
    melted and cooled

1. Preheat the oven to 350°.

2. Generously butter the entire inside of a 10-inch layer cake pan. Sprinkle 1 tablespoon of flour around the pan, tilt the pan from side to side to coat it evenly with the flour, then invert the pan and tap it to remove any excess flour.

3. Using an electric mixer, beat the eggs, sugar and vanilla extract together until the mixture triples in volume and runs off the beater in thick ribbons.

4. Add ⅓ cup of the remaining flour at a time, sprinkling it over the egg mixture and then folding it in with a large rubber spatula. Watch carefully for any pockets of dry flour and fold them in. Fold in the melted butter 2 tablespoons at a time.

5. Pour and scrape the cake batter into the prepared pan and bake on the middle rack of the oven for 30 to 35 minutes, or until the cake is a light golden brown and shrinks slightly from the sides of the pan. Remove the cake from the oven. Let it cool for 10 minutes before transferring it from the pan to a wire rack to cool completely.

Custard

2 tablespoons granulated
    sugar
1 tablespoon cornstarch
2 large egg yolks
2¼ cups milk
½ teaspoon vanilla extract

1. Place the sugar and cornstarch in a small heavy saucepan (not aluminum) and mix them together. With a small wire whisk, beat in the egg yolks until you have a smooth yellow paste. Gradually whisk in the milk in a thin stream to prevent lumps.

2. Place the saucepan on medium heat and stir with the whisk until the milk comes to a boil and thickens. Remove the pan from the heat and whisk in the vanilla extract. Pour into a storage container, cover with plastic wrap, and refrigerate until thoroughly chilled.

Filling and Decorations

1 cup raspberry preserves

1 cup dry sherry

1 cup sliced almonds, toasted

2 cups chilled heavy cream, whipped and flavored with 2 tablespoons confectioners' sugar

8 to 10 whole strawberries, washed and hulled

1. Slice the cake into 3 layers and let them dry out for a few hours. Spread the layers with the raspberry preserves and reassemble them, gently pressing them together.

2. Cut the filled layers into large cubes and put them into a deep glass serving bowl. Sprinkle with half of the sherry, toss the cubes, and sprinkle again with the remaining sherry. Mix in the toasted almonds, then the custard. Decorate the top with the whipped cream and strawberries.

MENU

Relish Tray

Baking Powder Biscuits (page 53)

Roast Fresh Ham

German Potato Salad

Beet and Onion Salad

Coleslaw

Chocolate Mousse

Relish Tray

The relish tray is pure American fare. It is very popular in New England and throughout the midwestern states. It is served in private homes as well as in many restaurants along with bread and butter at the beginning of a meal. Relishes are also commonly offered as part of a salad bar in restaurants all over the country.

A relish tray can consist of many different components, but here are a few suggestions: pickled onions, assorted olives, hearts of celery, candied kumquats, cucumber salad, cranberry-orange-nut relish (on page 120), pickled watermelon rind, and even cottage cheese.

Roast Fresh Ham

*One 8- to 10-pound fresh
   ham*
1 large garlic clove, peeled
2 tablespoons coarse salt
*½ teaspoon freshly ground
   pepper*
½ teaspoon thyme
1 cup white wine

1. Preheat the oven to 325°.

2. Slice the garlic lengthwise into thin slices.

3. Remove the skin from the ham and with the tip of a paring knife, make small incisions in the ham. Insert a slice of garlic into each slit.

4. Mix the salt, pepper, and thyme and rub the mixture into the surface of the meat. Place the ham on a rack in a large shallow roasting pan. Place the roasting pan on a rack in the lower part of the oven, and roast the ham, allowing 25 minutes per pound, or until a meat thermometer registers 170°. Halfway into the roasting period, add the wine to the pan and, from time to time, baste the meat with it.

5. When the ham is done, transfer it to a warm serving platter. Place the roasting pan on top of the stove over high heat and reduce any liquid to a glaze, scraping all the brown bits loose from the pan. Spoon the glaze over the ham before serving.

German Potato Salad

If you would like to serve American potato salad instead of the German version, omit the coleslaw, which also contains mayonnaise, from the menu.

YIELD: 8 TO 10 SERVINGS

5 pounds new potatoes
*1¼ cups finely chopped
   celery*
*1¼ cups finely chopped
   onions*
2 cups vegetable oil
¼ cup distilled white vinegar
1½ teaspoons salt
1 egg yolk
*½ teaspoon freshly ground
   white pepper*
¼ cup chopped parsley

1. Place the potatoes in a large pot and cover with cold water. Bring the water to a boil over high heat, and cook the potatoes until they are tender, about 10 to 14 minutes, depending on their size. Test for doneness by piercing them with the tip of a paring knife. Drain the potatoes in a colander and, when they are cool enough to handle, peel and cut them into ¼-inch-thick slices, letting the slices fall into a bowl. Stir in the chopped celery and onions.

2. In a small bowl and with a wire whisk, beat the oil, vinegar, salt, egg yolk, and pepper together, then pour the mixture over the potatoes and mix well. Toss the potato salad with the chopped parsley before serving.

American Potato Salad

Potatoes

YIELD: 8 TO 10 SERVINGS

5 pounds new potatoes
½ teaspoon salt
¼ cup distilled white vinegar
1¼ cups finely chopped celery
1¼ cups finely chopped onion
1½ cups finely chopped green pepper
¼ cup chopped parsley
½ teaspoon freshly ground pepper

1. Place the potatoes in a large pot and cover them with cold water. Bring the water to a boil over high heat, reduce the heat to medium, and cook the potatoes until they are tender, about 10 to 14 minutes depending on the size. Test the potatoes for doneness by piercing them with the tip of a paring knife. Drain the potatoes in a colander and, when they are cool enough to handle, peel and cut them into ¼-inch-thick slices, letting the slices fall into a large bowl.

2. Dissolve the salt in the vinegar and sprinkle the vinegar over the warm potatoes. Add the celery, onion, green pepper, and parsley, and gently stir all the ingredients together. Season with the pepper.

Mayonnaise Dressing

3 large egg yolks, at room temperature
1 teaspoon dry mustard
1 teaspoon salt
¾ teaspoon freshly ground white pepper
1 cup olive oil
1 cup vegetable oil
2 tablespoons lemon juice
4 hard-cooked eggs, coarsely chopped

1. With a whisk or an electric mixer, beat the egg yolks with the dry mustard, salt, and white pepper for 3 or 4 minutes, or until the egg yolks thicken.

2. Combine the olive and vegetable oils in a 2-cup measure. At medium speed, slowly incorporate 1 cup of the oil in a very fine stream. Continue beating, but more rapidly, until all of the oil has been incorporated. Add the lemon juice, and stir in the coarsely chopped egg.

3. Stir the mayonnaise dressing into the potato mixture with a rubber spatula until well blended. Cover the bowl with plastic wrap and refrigerate for at least 8 hours before serving.

Beet and Onion Salad

This beet and onion salad was a once-a-week treat when I was growing up. It is a festive addition to this New Year's buffet menu: Its red color looks especially fine next to a large bowl of potato salad.

YIELD: 8 TO 10 SERVINGS

3 pounds beets
2 onions, thinly sliced
1 teaspoon coriander seeds
6 whole cloves
1 pint distilled white
    vinegar
$\frac{1}{2}$ cup water
$\frac{1}{2}$ cup granulated sugar

1. Trim the tops from the beets, leaving on $\frac{1}{2}$ inch of the stems so the beets will retain more color while cooking. Cook the beets in boiling water until tender, about 15 to 20 minutes, depending on their size. Test for doneness with the point of a paring knife. When the beets are cool enough to handle, remove the skins and cut them into $\frac{1}{4}$-inch-thick slices, letting the slices fall into a large bowl.

2. Separate the onion slices into rings and mix them with the sliced beets.

3. Tie the coriander seeds and cloves in a piece of cheesecloth.

4. Combine the vinegar, water, and sugar in a saucepan and add the spices. Cook the mixture, stirring, over low heat until the sugar dissolves. Raise the heat, let the mixture boil for 5 minutes, and then pour it over the beets. When the liquid cools to room temperature, cover the beets with plastic wrap and refrigerate overnight. Before serving, remove and discard the cheesecloth with the spices.

Cole Slaw

YIELD: 8 TO 10 SERVINGS

$3\frac{1}{2}$ pounds cabbage
$1\frac{1}{2}$ cups mayonnaise
1 cup sour cream
2 teaspoons sugar
3 teaspoons dry mustard
$\frac{1}{4}$ cup chopped chives
1 tablespoon celery seeds
Salt and pepper to taste

1. Remove and discard the outer bruised leaves and the core of the cabbage. With a large knife, shred the cabbage very thinly and place it in a large bowl.

2. Mix all the remaining ingredients together and stir into the shredded cabbage. Taste for seasoning. Cover and refrigerate for several hours before serving.

Chocolate Mousse

YIELD: 8 TO 10 SERVINGS

8 ounces semisweet chocolate, chopped into small pieces
$\frac{1}{4}$ cup strong coffee
6 large egg yolks
$\frac{1}{2}$ cup granulated sugar
12 tablespoons unsalted butter (1$\frac{1}{2}$ sticks), softened
6 large egg whites
$\frac{3}{4}$ cup heavy cream, chilled
2 tablespoons confectioners' sugar

1. Place the chocolate and coffee in a heavy saucepan on very low heat. Stir occasionally and, as soon as the chocolate is melted, remove the pan from the heat and set aside.

2. Beat the egg yolks and the granulated sugar together until very thick and light in color.

3. Stir the chocolate-coffee mixture to make sure it is smooth, then beat it into the thickened egg yolks.

4. Beat the egg whites until they form firm but moist peaks. Stir about one-fourth of the egg whites into the chocolate mixture, then very gently fold in the remaining egg whites until no trace of white shows.

5. Pour the mousse into a 1$\frac{1}{2}$-quart serving bowl and refrigerate for at least 4 hours before serving.

6. Whip the cream with the confectioners' sugar until it holds firm peaks. Spoon the whipped cream into a pastry bag fitted with a number 4 or 5 star tube, and decorate the top of the mousse with swirls or rosettes. Sprinkle with additional chopped chocolate, or decorate with candied violets, or use both.

New Year's Day Open House

An open house is a wonderful way to welcome in the New Year and to entertain family and friends. The continuous arriving and leaving characteristic of an open house means that you can accommodate many people easily, and I also find that the constant exchanging of hellos and goodbyes adds to the festivity I love.

Don't be intimidated by the quantity of food suggested in the long menu. Remember that there are actually only two secrets to a successful New Year's Day open house: make all the preparations you can in advance, and never forget on New Year's Eve that you are entertaining on New Year's Day!

For the advance preparations, here are my suggestions. Make the vegetable soup weeks ahead and freeze it. The brioche can also be made weeks ahead and frozen; transfer it from the freezer to the refrigerator the night before the party. The duck pâté and the country pâté can be made four days ahead. The pickled halibut *must* be made three days ahead. Pesto mayonnaise can be prepared two to three days in advance. Unless you live in a humid climate, the croquembouche puffs can be made and assembled two days ahead and, covered with plastic wrap, kept at room temperature; they can then be filled a few hours before serving. You can even bake the ham two days early and on New Year's morning let it come to room temperature, apply the glaze, and put it in a 400° oven for five or ten minutes. The mustard dill sauce for the salmon and the cotechino can both be made the day before; remove the cotechino from the refrigerator early in the day.

The cassoulet, as is noted in the recipe, needs only to have its components assembled and baked on the day of the party. Its accompaniments are simplicity itself to prepare.

```
┌─────────────────────────────────────────────┐
│  ┌───────────────────────────────────────┐  │
│  │               MENU                     │  │
│  │        Smoked Salmon with              │  │
│  │        Mustard Dill Sauce              │  │
│  │                                        │  │
│  │   Old-fashioned Vegetable-Beef Soup    │  │
│  │                                        │  │
│  │    Baked Ham with Bourbon Peaches      │  │
│  │                                        │  │
│  │          Pickled Halibut               │  │
│  │                                        │  │
│  │            Duck Pâté                   │  │
│  │                                        │  │
│  │         Chicken Liver Pâté             │  │
│  │                                        │  │
│  │           Country Pâté                 │  │
│  │                                        │  │
│  │        Pesto Mayonnaise Dip            │  │
│  │                                        │  │
│  │         Cotechino Sausage              │  │
│  │                                        │  │
│  │           Brie in Brioche              │  │
│  │                                        │  │
│  │          Croquembouche                 │  │
│  └───────────────────────────────────────┘  │
└─────────────────────────────────────────────┘
```

Mustard Dill Sauce

YIELD: APPROXIMATELY 1½ CUPS

½ cup Dijon mustard
2 teaspoons dry mustard
¼ cup distilled white vinegar
⅔ cup vegetable oil
½ cup finely chopped fresh dill
2 tablespoons finely chopped fresh parsley

Mix all the ingredients thoroughly and let the sauce sit for 2 hours before serving. Serve with smoked salmon.

Old-fashioned Vegetable-Beef Soup

You can make this vegetable soup with the broth from the mincemeat recipe on page 7, using it to replace the cold water called for in the instructions below. If there is not enough broth to cover the bones and beef shin, add some water. In any case, leaving the skin on the onions in this recipe gives the broth a rich color. In addition to the vegetables called for here, you can use tiny cauliflower florets, green peas, and green beans cut into small pieces. Being a rice and noodle lover, I often add one or the other to the soup, too. Cook the noodles or rice separately in lightly salted boiling water so the starch doesn't cloud the broth.

YIELD: 10 TO 12 SERVINGS

3 pounds beef bones, cut into 1-inch-long pieces
3 pounds beef shin
1 tablespoon salt
2 teaspoons peppercorns
1 bay leaf
½ teaspoon thyme
2 sprigs parsley
A few fresh celery leaves
2 large yellow onions, with the skins left on and washed
3 leeks, cut crosswise into ¼-inch-thick rounds and thoroughly washed
3 carrots, thinly sliced
3 celery ribs, coarsely chopped
2 small white turnips, coarsely diced
2 onions, peeled and coarsely chopped

1. Place the bones and beef shin in an 8- to 10-quart pot and cover them with cold water. Bring the liquid to a boil over high heat, reduce the heat and simmer for 10 minutes. Using a large slotted spoon, skim off all the foam that rises to the top of the broth. Add the salt, peppercorns, bay leaf, thyme, parsley sprigs, celery leaves, and yellow onions. Continue to simmer the broth, partially covered, for 3 hours.

2. Transfer the beef shin to a plate and set it aside. Remove the bones, yellow onions, parsley, and celery leaves and discard them. Return the broth to a boil, and with a large spoon, skim the fat from its surface.

3. Add all the remaining vegetables and return the broth to a boil. Reduce the heat and continue to simmer the soup for 30 minutes, or until the vegetables are cooked.

4. Trim any fat from the beef shin and cut the meat into small cubes. When the vegetables have cooked, return the meat to the pot. Bring the soup to a boil and serve.

Baked Ham with Bourbon Peaches

If the baking time I have given for the ham seems excessive, it is for a good reason. Precooked hams are injected with a brine that makes the ham very moist. This is not really a desirable characteristic. By increasing the baking time, this moisture is evaporated, giving the meat a texture similar to that of an aged country ham.

YIELD: 10 TO 12 SERVINGS

One 10- to 12-pound
   precooked ham
1 cup brown sugar
1 tablespoon dry mustard
2 tablespoons unsalted
   butter
12 fresh or canned peach
   halves
$\frac{1}{2}$ cup bourbon

1. Preheat the oven to 325°.

2. Scrub the ham under cold running water and pat it dry with paper towels. Place the ham, skin side up, on a rack in a shallow roasting pan and bake it as close to the middle of the oven as possible for 5 hours.

3. Remove the ham from the oven and, when it is cool enough to handle, cut off and discard the rind and all but $\frac{1}{4}$ inch of the fat.

4. Place the sugar and dry mustard in a small sieve and, with a wooden spoon, push the mixture through the sieve so that it covers the top of the ham evenly.

5. Increase the oven temperature to 400° and return the ham to the oven. Continue to bake it for an additional 5 to 10 minutes, or until the sugar melts into a glaze.

6. Reduce the oven temperature to 350°. Spread the butter on the bottom of a large shallow ovenproof dish. Place the peach halves in the dish, flat side down and in one layer. Pour the bourbon into a small saucepan and place the pan over low heat. When the bourbon is warm, remove the pan from the heat and carefully ignite the liquor with a match. Pour the bourbon over the peaches, then bake them in the oven for 20 minutes, basting every 5 minutes with the bourbon and butter.

7. Serve the ham together with the peaches on a large heated meat platter.

Pickled Halibut

This wonderful Portuguese fish dish must be prepared three days before serving. I have included it in small and large buffets, served it for lunch, and very often used it as a first course. Garnished with small new potatoes (boiled, peeled, and cooled to room temperature), hard-cooked eggs, black olives, and sprigs of fresh coriander, it makes a superb first course or even a meal. I promise that whenever you serve it and however you garnish it, the pickled halibut will always bring raves from your guests.

YIELD: 8 SERVINGS

1¼ cups olive oil
2 pounds halibut, cut into ¾-inch-thick steaks
1 cup flour
2 large onions, thinly sliced
2 bay leaves
4 medium-sized carrots, coarsely grated
1 cup white wine vinegar
½ cup white wine
2½ teaspoons finely chopped garlic
2½ teaspoons salt
¼ teaspoon dried hot red pepper flakes, crushed
¼ teaspoon freshly ground white pepper

1. In a large heavy skillet that is not aluminum or iron, heat ⅓ cup of the olive oil. Dredge the halibut steaks in the flour, shake them lightly, and place them in hot oil. Cook the steaks about 5 minutes on each side, or until golden brown, and remove them to paper towels to drain and cool.

2. Wash and dry the skillet thoroughly and heat the remaining oil in it. Cook the onions until soft and translucent, then stir in all the remaining ingredients and cook for an additional 5 minutes.

3. Remove the skin and bones from the fish. Spread one third of the vegetable mixture over the bottom of an 8-by-12-inch serving dish, and place half of the steaks on top. Spread half of the remaining vegetable mixture on top of the fish. Make a second layer of fish, and cover it with all the remaining vegetables and liquid in the skillet.

4. When the contents of the dish have cooled to room temperature, cover with plastic wrap (not foil, which does not seal well enough) and marinate in the refrigerator for 3 days. Remove the halibut from the refrigerator at least 2 hours before serving.

Duck Pâté

*One 5- to 6-pound duck,
   skinned and boned*
3 tablespoons butter
*½ cup finely chopped
   shallots*
*1½ teaspoon finely chopped
   garlic*
1 pound lean ground pork
*½ pound ground pork
   fatback*
¾ cup cognac
2 large eggs
1 tablespoon salt
*½ teaspoon freshly ground
   white pepper*
½ teaspoon thyme
½ teaspoon allspice
*⅛ teaspoon saltpeter
   (available in drugstores)*
3 chicken livers
*1½ pounds fresh pork
   fatback, cut into ⅛-inch-
   thick slices*
2 bay leaves

1. Remove one breast half from the duck and set it aside. Coarsely chop all the remaining meat.

2. Melt the butter in a medium-sized skillet, add the shallots and garlic, and cook for 3 minutes. Scrape them into a small bowl and set aside.

3. In a large mixing bowl, combine the chopped duck meat, ground pork, and fatback together with ½ cup of the cognac, the eggs, salt, pepper, thyme, allspice and saltpeter. Add the cooked shallots and garlic and, with your hands, mix all the ingredients together. Cover the bowl with plastic wrap and refrigerate for 3 days.

4. Cut the reserved duck breast meat into 8 long strips and place the strips in a small bowl together with the chicken livers. Add the remaining ¼ cup of cognac. Cover with plastic wrap and refrigerate for 3 days.

5. Pound the slices of pork fatback between two sheets of wax paper until the pork fat is very thin.

6. Line the bottom and sides of a 1½-quart oval pâté dish with overlapping slices of the fatback. Reserve enough slices to cover the top of the pâté.

7. Preheat the oven to 350°.

8. Pack one third of the ground meat mixture into the lined dish. Place 4 strips of the duck breast lengthwise on top of the ground meat. Spread a thin layer of the ground meat mixture on top of the strips. Set the chicken and duck livers in a line down the center of the pâté. Pack a layer of the ground meat mixture on top of the livers. As before, place the remaining 4 strips of the duck breast over the top. Pack the remaining ground meat mixture into the dish and cover with the remaining slices of the fatback. Place the 2 bay leaves on top and cover the dish.

9. Place the pâté dish in a roasting pan, and bring a pot of water to a boil. Place a rack at the middle of the oven, pull it partway out, and place the roasting pan on it. Pour enough boiling water into the pan to come halfway up the sides of the pâté dish. Slide the rack back into the oven and bake

the pâté for 1½ hours. Let the pâté cool to room temperature before refrigerating.

Chicken Liver Pâté

Although this pâté is made with chicken livers, the texture is very close to that of a goose liver pâté.

Pâté

YIELD: ABOUT 6 CUPS

¾ pound unsalted butter (3 sticks), plus 8 tablespoons unsalted butter (1 stick)
1 cup finely chopped onions
1 clove garlic, finely chopped
2 pounds chicken livers
¾ cup applejack
1 tablespoon salt
¼ teaspoon white pepper
1½ teaspoons lemon juice

1. Heat 4 tablespoons of the butter in a large heavy skillet, add the onions and garlic, and cook over medium heat for about 5 minutes, or until the onions are lightly colored. Transfer the mixture to the container of a food processor.

2. Wash and dry the skillet thoroughly, add 4 more tablespoons of the butter, and set the skillet over high heat. When the butter is very hot, add the chicken livers and toss them around in the hot butter until they become brown on the outside. Remove the pan from the heat, pour in the applejack, and carefully ignite it with a match.

3. Add the chicken livers, salt, and pepper to the container of the food processor. Process the onion-liver mixture until it is a smooth purée. Let the mixture sit in the container until it cools to room temperature.

4. Remove ½ pound of chilled butter from the refrigerator and tap it with a rolling pin to soften it while keeping it cold and non-oily. Process or grind the cooled chicken livers with the butter until well blended. Add the lemon juice and taste for seasoning. Scrape the chicken-liver mixture into a six-cup crock or glass serving dish, pour the aspic (below) over it, cover with plastic wrap, and store in the refrigerator until firm.

Aspic

¾ cup chicken broth
1 teaspoon gelatin

Pour the chicken broth into a small heatproof bowl and sprinkle the gelatin over the top. When the gelatin has softened, set the bowl in a pan of simmering water and stir over low heat until the gelatin dissolves. Remove the pan from the heat and set the bowl of aspic over ice. Stir until the aspic becomes syrupy, then pour it over the pâté.

Country Pâté

A flavorful country pâté is always a favorite at cocktail parties, as a first course for a dinner, or even as a simple lunch served with German or American potato salad (page 139 and page 140). Mixing the ingredients, or forcemeat, for the pâté thoroughly will ensure good flavor. The best way to do this is by hand, but dip your hands in cold water first to keep the forcemeat from sticking to them. Before serving, let the pâté sit in the refrigerator for two days to let the flavors develop.

YIELD: 10 TO 12 SERVINGS

3 tablespoons unsalted butter
1 cup finely chopped onions
2½ teaspoons finely chopped garlic
1 pound lean ground pork
1 pound lean ground veal
1 pound fatback ground pork, plus 1 pound pork fatback, very thinly sliced by the butcher
¼ cup brandy
3 eggs
2½ teaspoons salt
½ teaspoon freshly ground pepper
½ teaspoon crumbled thyme
½ teaspoon allspice
⅛ teaspoon saltpeter (available at drug stores)
2 bay leaves

1. Melt the butter in a medium-sized skillet, add the onions, and cook until they are translucent. Add the garlic and cook for 2 minutes longer, but do not let the onions color. Scrape the onions and garlic into a small mixing bowl and let them cool.

2. Place the ground pork, veal, ground fatback, brandy, eggs, salt, pepper, thyme, allspice, and saltpeter in a large mixing bowl. Add the onions and garlic and, with your hands, mix all the ingredients together.

3. Cover the bowl with plastic wrap and refrigerate for 3 days.

4. Preheat the oven to 350°.

5. Line a 10-by-4-by-3-inch pâté dish with the thinly sliced fatback, reserving enough slices to cover the top of the pâté.

6. Pack the pâté mixture into the lined mold, cover with the remaining sliced fatback, and top with the 2 bay leaves.

7. Set the pâté dish in a roasting pan, and bring a pot of water to a boil. Pull out the middle rack of the oven partway, place the roasting pan on it and pour enough boiling water into the roasting pan to come halfway up the sides of the pâté dish. Slide the rack back into the oven and bake the pâté for 1½ hours.

8. Remove the pâté dish from the pan, and let the pâté cool to room temperature before storing it in the refrigerator.

Pesto Mayonnaise Dip

If fresh basil is not available in your local market, you should be able to find it in a gourmet market. Alternatively, some very good pesto sauces are sold commercially in 8-ounce containers, the amount required for this recipe. They are usually located in the frozen food department. Simply mix the defrosted pesto sauce with the mayonnaise.

YIELD: ABOUT 2 CUPS

1 cup of firmly packed
    fresh basil leaves
$\frac{1}{2}$ teaspoon salt
1 clove garlic, finely
    chopped
2 tablespoons walnuts
$\frac{1}{4}$ cup freshly grated
    Parmesan cheese
$\frac{1}{4}$ cup olive oil
1 cup mayonnaise
    (preferably homemade)

Place the basil, salt, garlic, walnuts, and Parmesan cheese in the container of a food processor and purée them, then add the oil. Scrape the mixture into a medium-sized bowl and fold in the mayonnaise. Taste for salt and pepper. Refrigerate for several hours before serving. Serve as a dip with a variety of fresh vegetables.

Cotechino Sausage

Cotechino, with its wonderful coarse texture and garlic flavor, is not only a great contribution to the cassoulet on pages 156–158, it can also be a very satisfying luncheon dish. However, if this Italian sausage is not available, substitute any garlic-flavored pork sausage, such as kielbasa.

One 1- to $1\frac{1}{2}$-pound
    cotechino sausage

1. Prick the sausage with the tip of a paring knife in several places.

2. Place the sausage in a large saucepan and cover it with cold water. Bring the water to a boil. Reduce the heat, and simmer the sausage for 45 minutes.

3. Let the sausage cool in the liquid and, as soon as it is cool enough to handle, remove the skin.

3. Serve warm or at room temperature, sliced or unsliced.

Brie in Brioche

Although Brie is a dessert cheese, it is often served with drinks before dinner. Baked in beautiful brioche casing, it makes a splendid and unusual addition to a buffet as well. This excellent combination is also a very popular brunch dish at my restaurant, where I accompany it with a tossed green salad. Unlike the familiar spongelike brioche, this brioche is dense enough to contain the bubbly hot cheese at its interior. To prevent the cheese from running out of the loaf once the first servings have been made, try the following. Make a three-inch-wide strip of doubled aluminum foil and lightly butter one side of the strip. Press the buttered side against the exposed cheese until you are ready to cut into the loaf again.

YIELD: 8 TO 10 SERVINGS

2 packages active dry yeast
3 tablespoons, plus $\frac{1}{2}$ teaspoon, sugar
$\frac{3}{4}$ cup milk, brought to a boil and allowed to cool to 110° to 115°
$4\frac{1}{2}$ cups all-purpose flour
2 teaspoons salt
6 large eggs
$\frac{1}{2}$ pound unsalted butter (2 sticks), softened
1 ripe 2-pound Brie, chilled and carefully trimmed of its skin
3 beaten egg yolks

1. Stir the yeast and the $\frac{1}{2}$ teaspoon sugar into the warm milk. Let the mixture stand until it foams, about 4 to 6 minutes.

2. In a large bowl, combine the remaining 3 tablespoons sugar, the flour, salt, eggs, softened butter, and yeast-milk mixture. Stir all the ingredients together until the milk is absorbed by the flour. Remove the dough from the bowl and place it on a lightly floured surface.

3. Knead the dough by pushing it forward and folding it back in half on top of itself. Continue to knead the dough for 10 to 15 minutes, or until it is smooth and elastic. When necessary, sprinkle the dough with enough flour to keep it from sticking to your hands and the work surface.

4. Place the dough in a large buttered bowl and turn it to coat it with butter. Cover the dough with plastic wrap or a towel and let it rise for $1\frac{1}{2}$ hours, or until double in size. When the dough has doubled in size, punch it down, cover it, and place it in the refrigerator. Chill for 1 hour.

5. On a lightly floured surface, roll out one half of the dough to a thickness of $\frac{1}{4}$ inch. Transfer the dough to a buttered cookie sheet. Place the Brie at the center of the dough and, with a small knife or pastry wheel, trim the brioche, leaving a $1\frac{1}{2}$-inch border around the cheese. Fold the edge of the brioche up and over the top of the Brie, pressing the brioche against the cheese. (See the illustration on page 153.)

6. Roll out the remaining half of the dough as before and, with a pastry brush, coat the top with the beaten egg yolk. Drape the dough over the Brie, egg-wash side down, and press it against the top of the cheese and the other layer of brioche. Trim the top layer of dough along the base of the Brie, cutting through to the cookie sheet to create a neat package.

7. Brush the entire surface of the brioche with the egg-wash and, using the scraps of dough, decorate the brioche with any design you wish. Brush with the egg-wash again and let the dough rest for 30 minutes at room temperature before baking.

8. Preheat the oven to 350°.

9. Bake the brioche on a rack in the middle of the oven for 30 minutes, or until it is a dark golden brown. Transfer the loaf to a wire rack and let it rest for 2 hours before slicing.

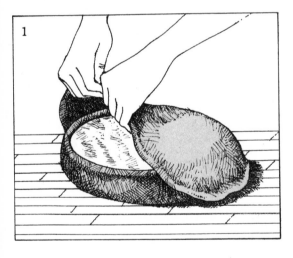

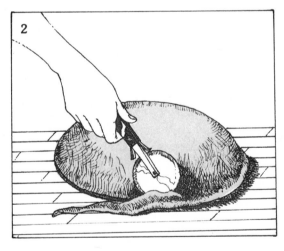

Assembling the Brie in brioche. *Place the Brie at the center of a rolled-out circle of brioche dough and fold the edges of the dough over the top edge of the cheese. Brush the top of another circle of brioche dough with* *beaten egg yolk; then place the dough over the Brie, brushed side down, pressing it against the first layer of brioche (1). Using a pastry cutter, trim off the excess dough (2).*

Croquembouche

A croquembouche may seem to be an impossible architectural feat, but the cream puffs and caramel of which it is constructed are really very simple to make. Not only that, the cream puff cases can be finished several weeks in advance and stored in the freezer. Before assembling the croquembouche, simply place the puffs in a 400° oven for 10 minutes to restore their freshly baked flavor. This *pâte à choux* (cream puff pastry) is made with half milk and half water instead of with all water to make the walls of the puffs stronger. If a croquembouche mold is not available, make a 14-inch high conical form with a 9-inch-wide base out of cardboard, staple or tape it together, and cover it with aluminum foil. To make the croquembouche resemble a Christmas tree even more, you may decorate the pastry with pieces of red candied cherries and/or green angelica (see the second color section). Candied violets also make attractive decorations. Simply dip one side of the decorations of your choice in the caramel and stick them at random on the pastry.

YIELD: 18 TO 24 SERVINGS

$2\frac{3}{4}$ cups water
$\frac{3}{4}$ cup milk
$\frac{1}{2}$ teaspoon salt
2 teaspoons, plus 5 cups, sugar
12 tablespoons butter, cut into small bits
$1\frac{1}{2}$ cups all-purpose flour
8 large eggs
$\frac{1}{2}$ teaspoon cream of tartar
3 cups heavy cream, chilled
$\frac{1}{4}$ cup confectioners' sugar
$1\frac{1}{2}$ teaspoons vanilla extract

1. Preheat the oven to 400° and lightly butter and flour two cookie sheets.

2. Measure the flour and sift it onto a piece of wax paper.

3. In a medium-sized saucepan, combine the water, milk, salt, 2 teaspoons of sugar, and butter. Bring the mixture to a boil over high heat and, when the butter has melted, add the flour all at once. Reduce the heat to medium and beat the dough mixture with a wooden spoon until it leaves the sides of the pan and forms a ball. Remove from the heat and let the dough sit for 5 minutes.

4. Beat in the eggs two at a time until they are thoroughly incorporated and the dough is smooth and shiny.

5. Fit a large pastry bag with a number 4 plain pastry tube. Fill the bag one-third full with the dough and twist the empty top closed.

6. Cup the bag in one hand, squeeze firmly, and with the other hand as a guide, shape the pastry into mounds that are $1\frac{1}{4}$ inches in diameter, $\frac{3}{4}$ inch high and spaced 2 inches apart. To obtain the proper shape, first outline the base, then continuing in a spiral motion, fill in the base and build up the top.

7. Bake the cream puffs on a rack in the middle of the oven for 25 to 30 minutes, or until they are a deep golden brown. Transfer the puffs to a wire rack to cool. Continue to make additional puffs until all the dough has been baked.

8. Place $2\frac{1}{2}$ cups of the remaining sugar and 1 cup of the water in a medium-sized saucepan and cook over low heat until the sugar dissolves. Mix the cream of tartar with a little water and add it to the syrup. With a clean natural bristle pastry brush and cold water, brush the sides of the pan above the level of the syrup to keep crystals from forming on the pan. Raise the heat to high and cook the syrup to the hard crack stage, or 290° on a candy thermometer. Set a shallow pan of warm water large enough to hold the saucepan nearby, and when the syrup is ready, put the saucepan in it to stop the syrup from cooking and to keep it fluid for a while.

9. One by one, hold each puff by the bottom and dip the top in the caramel, then gently slide it against the edge of the saucepan to remove the excess caramel. Set the puff on a piece of wax paper. If the puffs tip over don't worry, they won't stick to the wax paper. If the caramel gets too thick, return it to medium heat until it becomes fluid again.

10. With a pastry brush, lightly coat a croquembouche mold with flavorless vegetable oil.

11. To assemble the croquembouche, make a second batch of caramel using the remaining $2\frac{1}{2}$ cups of sugar and set it in warm water. Dip each puff in the caramel again, but this time coat one side. Then, starting at the base of the mold, stick the cream puffs together, building around and up the conical-shaped mold until the entire surface is completely covered with puffs.

12. When ready to serve the croquembouche, pierce a pencil-sized hole in the side of each puff. Then whip the heavy cream together with the confectioners' sugar and vanilla extract in a chilled bowl at medium speed. Using a large pastry bag fitted with a number 4 plain pastry tube fill each puff with the whipped cream.

Caviar Dip with Cucumber Sticks

YIELD: 2 CUPS OF DIP

1 cup yogurt
1 cup sour cream
2 tablespoons chopped
   fresh dill weed
¼ cup chopped chives
2 tablespoons chopped
   parsley
Dash of Tabasco sauce
8 ounces red caviar
3 cucumbers

1. Combine the yogurt, sour cream, dill, chives, parsley, and Tabasco sauce. Mix until the ingredients are well blended. With a rubber spatula, gently fold in the caviar. Refrigerate for at least 2 hours before serving.

2. Peel the cucumbers and cut them in half lengthwise. Using a teaspoon, scoop out the seeds. Cut each cucumber in half across the center, making 12 pieces, then cut each piece lengthwise into 4 sticks. Place the cucumber sticks in a colander and sprinkle them lightly with salt. Let them sit for 30 minutes to extract some of their water. Pat the sticks dry with paper towels and chill in the refrigerator. Before serving, arrange them attractively around the bowl of dip.

Cassoulet

Cassoulet is a French peasant dish that became the rage in New York in the mid-1950s. At one point during that period, I catered through the winter months and sometimes served it to as many as 125 people. The dish lends itself to large groups of people and it's great when the weather is cold.

Originally made from leftovers, cassoulet has always contained several types of meats. Goose, lamb and/or pork and a garlic-flavored sausage are classic, but in this recipe, duck has been substituted for the goose. Plenty of red wine and loaves of French bread are perfect accompaniments.

Even though the recipe is quite long and involves many ingredients, cooking the component parts can be started several days before a party, at your leisure, and the parts can be refrigerated separately. The final step of assembling the cassoulet can be easily accomplished the afternoon of the party. To increase the number of servings, simply double or triple the recipe.

YIELD: 8 TO 10 SERVINGS

4 cups navy beans (2 pounds)
1 pound lean salt pork
4 cups chicken broth, fresh or canned
2 large onions, peeled
2 cups canned tomatoes, drained and coarsely chopped
1 carrot, scraped
2 cloves garlic, bruised
2 teaspoons salt
2 bay leaves
4 sprigs parsley
1½ pounds fresh pork butt
1½ pounds boned shoulder of lamb
½ cup dry red wine
1 cotechino sausage, cooked as directed on page 151
One 5- to 6-pound duck, roasted as directed on page 124
2 cups fresh bread crumbs
½ cup chopped parsley

1. Soak the beans in a large bowl with enough water to cover for 3 to 4 hours.

2. Simmer the salt pork in a medium-sized saucepan with enough water to cover for 15 minutes. Drain and set aside.

3. Drain the beans and place them in an 8- to 10-quart casserole. Add the chicken broth and enough cold water to cover the beans by about 2 inches. Bring the liquid to a boil over high heat and skim the foam off with a slotted spoon. Add the salt pork, onions, tomatoes, carrot, garlic, salt, bay leaves, and parsley sprigs. Cook for about 1½ hours, or until the beans are tender. If necessary, add additional water.

4. Strain the liquid from the beans through a colander into a large mixing bowl and set aside. Place the beans in another bowl and discard the onions, carrot, bay leaves, and parsley sprigs. Set the beans aside.

5. Preheat the oven to 350°.

6. Salt and pepper the pork butt and the shoulder of lamb. Place them in a large shallow roasting pan and roast on a rack in the middle of the oven for 1 hour. Remove the lamb shoulder and continue to roast the pork butt for an additional 30 minutes. In a small bowl, reserve ¼ cup of the fat from the pan and discard the rest. Place the roasting pan over medium heat and deglaze the pan with the red wine, scraping all the brown bits from the bottom and sides of the pan. Stir this meat glaze into the beans.

7. Cut the skinned cotechino into ½-thick slices. Quarter the duck. Cut the legs and thighs into 8 pieces, and each breast half into 4 pieces. Cut the pork butt and lamb shoulder into 1-inch chunks.

8. Place one-third of the beans on the bottom of a large shallow casserole. Layer one-half of the assorted meats on

top. Place the second one-third of the beans on top of the meat. Make another layer of the remaining meats and cover with the remaining beans.

9. Taste the stock for salt, then pour it into the casserole until it almost covers the beans. Spread the bread crumbs evenly over the top of the casserole and dribble them with the reserved pork fat.

10. Set the casserole over high heat until the liquid comes to a boil, then place it on a rack in the middle of the oven. Bake the cassoulet for $1\frac{1}{4}$ to $1\frac{1}{2}$ hours, or until the bread crumbs are a dark crusty brown.

11. Let the cassoulet rest for 15 to 20 minutes. Just before serving, sprinkle with the chopped parsley.

Fruit and Onion Salad

I have chosen this salad to follow the cassoulet because the fresh taste of the chilled grapefruit and orange sections and the refreshing quality of the salad dressing, which calls for grapefruit juice and orange juice instead of vinegar, create a satisfying prelude to the cheese dessert.

YIELD: 8 TO 10 SERVINGS

1 grapefruit
3 oranges
$\frac{3}{4}$ cup olive oil
2 tablespoons grapefruit
   juice
2 tablespoons orange juice
1 teaspoon dry mustard
1 teaspoon salt
$\frac{1}{2}$ teaspoon freshly ground
   pepper
1 large head of romaine
   lettuce
1 large red onion, peeled
   and thinly sliced

1. Section the oranges and grapefruit as instructed in the recipe for shrimp curry condiments, page 77.

2. In a small bowl, mix the olive oil, grapefruit juice, orange juice, pepper, salt, and mustard and set aside.

3. Remove any damaged or wilted outer leaves from the lettuce and tear the rest into medium-sized pieces. Wash the greens, drain them in a colander, and dry them with paper towels or spin them dry in a salad drier. Place them in a large salad bowl.

4. Scatter the onion slices over the greens, add the fruit sections, and toss together with the olive oil dressing.

A

Almond cake, 42–43
Almond crescents, 18–19
Almond glaze, 15
Anchovy dip, hot cream and, 65
Anise cookies, 20
Apple tart, open-faced, 95
Aspic, 149

B

Baked ham with bourbon peaches, 146
Baking powder biscuits, 53
Bay scallop ceviche, 65
Beard, James, 7
Beef, shell roast of, 133
Beef, standing rib roast, 116
Beer, 76
Beet and onion salad, 141
Beverages, 61, 68–71
  beer, 76
  for brunch, 87
  champagne punch, 69
  holiday eggnogg, 68
  hot buttered rum, 71
  hot toddy, 71
  mimosa, 69, 87
  Tom and Jerry, 70
  wassail, 70
  wine, 76
Biscuits, baking powder, 53
Boiled rice, 78
Breads
  baking powder biscuits, 53
  brioche, 28
    breakfast cake, 29–30
  poppy seed wreath, 32–33
  stollen, 44–45
  white, 46
  whole wheat, 47
Breakfast menus, Christmas Day, 111–113
Brie in brioche, 152–153
Brioche, 28
  breakfast cake, 29–30
  brie in, 152–153
Broccoli florets, 122
Broccoli purée, mushroom caps with, 134–135

Broiled grapefruit, 112
Brunch menus, 87–89
Brussel sprouts with chestnuts, 129
Buffet menus
  Christmas Eve, 101–110
  New Year's Eve, 131–142
Butter cake, German, 52–53
Butter cream
  mocha, 36
  for walnut cake, 39–40

C

Cabbage, red, 128
Cakes
  Christmas log with mocha butter cream, 35–38
  fruit
    golden, 6–7
    old-fashioned dark, 4–5
    Scotch black bun, 8–9
  German butter, 52–53
  King's, 50–51
  panettone, 41–42
  pithiviers, 42–43
  star of Zurich, 48–49
  strawberry cream roll, 105
  trifle, 135–136
  walnut, 39–40
Canapés and hors d'oeuvres
  bay scallop ceviche, 65
  caviar dip with cucumber sticks, 156
  crabmeat-turnip canapé, 63
  cucumber boats with shrimp, 67
  endive with cream cheese and caviar, 66
  hot clam and cheese canapés, 63
  hot cream and anchovy dip, 65
  irresistible roasted pecans, 64
  mignonette sauce, 62
  mushroom caps stuffed with chicken, 68
  onion drums, 66
  pesto mayonnaise dip, 151
  pickled shrimp, 62
  smoked salmon–cheese spread, 64
Candied grapefruit peel, 57
Candies, 55–60
  candied grapefruit peel, 57
  caramel popcorn balls, 56

Candies (*cont.*)
chocolate truffles, 137
divinity, 56
fondant, 60
marzipan fruit, 58–59
mixed nut crunch, 57
Caramel popcorn balls, 60
Cassoulet, 156–158
Caviar, endive with cream cheese and, 66
Caviar dip with cucumber sticks, 156
Celery remoulade, 81
Celery root and potatoes, purée of, 117
Champagne punch, 69
Cheese, cream, endive and caviar with, 66
Cheese canapés, hot clam and, 63
Cheese spread, smoked salmon , 64
Cherry tomatoes with basil, 134
Chestnut Bavarian cream, 91
Chestnuts, Brussels sprouts with, 129
Chicken, mushrooms stuffed with, 68
Chicken liver pâté, 149
Chicken livers and mushrooms in choux puff pastry, 89–90
Chocolate-covered fondant, 60
Chocolate mousse, 142
Chocolate truffles, 137
Christmas Day breakfast menu, 111–113
Christmas Eve buffet menus, 101–110
Christmas log with mocha butter cream, 35–38
Clams, hot, and cheese canapés, 63
Clams, mignonette sauce with, 62
Coach House plum pudding, 10–11
Cold lime soufflé, 80
Cole slaw, 141
Condiments, for curried shrimp, 77–78
Consommé Bellevue, 92
Consommé with marrow balls, 125–126
Cookies, 13–25
almond crescents, 18–19
anise, 20
Evelyn's Christmas, 18
hazelnut, 21
Jeanne Clancy's nut balls, 21
lebkuchen, 14–15
Lucia gingersnaps, 25
Moravian cutouts, 22
pfeffernusse, 15

St. Nicholas spice, 23
spiced Christmas trees, 16
spiced mushroom, 17
springerle, 24–25
spritz, 19
walnut balls, 20
wasps' nests, 16
Cotechino sausage, 151
Country pâté, 150
Crabmeat-turnip canapé, 63
Cranberry juice with ginger ale, 61
Cranberry mousse, 84–85
Cranberry-orange-nut relish, 120
Cranberry sauce, 120
Cream
chestnut Bavarian, 91
hot, and anchovy dip, 65
Cream cheese, with endive and caviar, 66
Creamed spinach, 83
Crisp potato pancakes, 83–84
Croquembouche, 154–155
Cucumber boats with shrimp, 67
Cucumber sticks, caviar dip with, 156
Curried shrimp, 76–78
Custard, in trifle, 136

D

Darr, Sally, 4
David, Elizabeth, 8
Dill, Evelyn, 18
Dinner menus, traditional, 115–129
American, 118–124
English, 116–117
German, 125–129
Divinity, 56
Dressing, mayonnaise, for American potato salad, 140
Drinks. *See Beverages*
Duck pâté, 148–149
Ducks, roast, with quince, 123–124

E

Egg cake, ratatouille, 92–94
Eggnogg, holiday, 68
Eggs, shirred, 111

Endive with cream cheese and caviar, 66
Endive salad, 99
Evelyn's Christmas cookies, 18

F

Finnan haddie roulade with mustard sauce, 97–98
Fondant candies, 60
French roast potatoes, 133
Fruit, marzipan, 58–59
Fruit and onion salad, 158
Fruitcake,
    Golden, 6–7
    Old-fashioned dark, 4–5
    Scotch black bun, 8–9

G

Garlic-flavored vinaigrette, 79
Garnish, for potato and leek soup, 88–89
German butter cake, 52–53
German potato salad, 139
Ginger ale with cranberry juice, 61
Gingersnaps, Lucia, 25
Glaze
    Almond, 15
    Fruitcake, 5
    Lebkuchen, 15
    Coach House plum pudding, 11
Glazed onions, 103
Golden fruitcake, 6–7
Goose, roast, with pears and prunes, 126–127
Grapefruit, broiled, 112
Grapefruit peel, candied, 57
Gratin potatoes, 104
Gravy, for roasted turkey, 119
Green bean salad, 108
Green beans, 122

H

Halibut, pickled, 147
Ham, baked, with bourbon peaches, 146
Ham, roast fresh, 139
Hard sauce, 11
Hash, Swedish, 113

Hazelnut cookies, 21
Holiday eggnogg, 68
Holiday mincemeat, 7
Hors d'oeuvres. *See* Canapés and hor d'oeuvres
Hot buttered rum, 71
Hot clam and cheese canapés, 63
Hot cream and anchovy dip, 65
Hot toddy, 71

I

Icing
    for Moravian cutouts, 24
    royal, 24
    for spiced mushroom cookies, 17
Irresistible roasted pecans, 64

J

Jeanne Clancy's nut balls, 21
Jelly, wine, 129

K

King's cake, 50–51

L

Lanigan, Anne, 15
Lebkuchen, 14–15
Leek soup, and potato, 88–89
Lemon meringue pie, 109–110
Lianidies, Leon, 10
Lime soufflé, cold, 80
Liver, chicken, pâté, 149
Livers, chicken, and mushrooms in choux puff
    pastry, 89–90
Lobster Newberg, 107
Lucia gingersnaps, 25

M

Madiera, prunes in, 127
Marrow balls, and consommé, 125–126
Marzipan fruit, 58–59
Marzipan walnut, 40

Mashed potatoes, 120
Mashed yellow turnips, 120
Mayonnaise dressing, for American potato salad, 140
Menus, holiday, 73–158
    brunch, 87–99
    Christmas Day breakfast, 111–113
    Christmas Eve buffet, 101–110
    New Year's Day open house, 143–158
    New Year's Eve buffet, 131–142
    party, 75–85
    traditional dinners, 115–129
Meringue mushrooms, 36–37
Mignonette sauce, 62
Mimosa, 69, 87
Mincemeat, holiday, 7
Mincemeat tartletts, 34–35
Mints, fondant, 60
Mixed green salad with garlic-flavored vinaigrette, 79
Mixed nut crunch, 57
Mocha butter cream, 36
Moravian cutouts, 22
Mousse, chocolate, 142
Mousse, cranberry, 84–85
Mushroom caps, with broccoli purée, 134–135
Mushroom-filled puff pastry, 106–107
Mushrooms, marzipan, 58
Mushrooms, pickled, 96
Mushrooms stuffed with chicken, 68
Mustard dill sauce, 144
Mustard sauce, 98

N
New Year's Day open house menus, 143–158
New Year's Eve buffet menus, 131–142
Nut balls
    Jeanne Clancy's, 21
    walnut, 20
Nut crunch, mixed, 57

O
Old-fashioned dark fruitcake, 4–5
Old-fashioned vegetable-beef soup, 145
Onion and beet salad, 141

Onion drums, 66
Onion salad, fruit and, 158
Onions, glazed, 103
Open-faced apple tart, 95
Orange-cranberry-nut relish, 120
Oysters, mignonette sauce with, 62

P
Pancakes, potato, 83–84
Panettone, 41–42
Party menus, Christmas, 75–85
Pastry, puff, 30–32
Pastry cone, paper, 38
Pastry leaves, 9
Pâté, chicken liver, 149
Pâté, country, 150
Pâté, duck, 148–149
Pears, poached, 127
Peas, sautéed snow, 103
Pecans, roasted, 64
Pesto mayonnaise dip, 151
Pfeffernusse, 15
Pickled halibut, 147
Pickled mushrooms, 96
Pickled shrimp, 62
Pie, lemon meringue, 109–110
Pilaf, rice, 108
Pithiviers, 42–43
Plum pudding, Coach House, 10–11
Poached pears, 127
Popadams, 79
Popcorn balls, caramel, 60
Poppy seed wreath, 32–33
Potato and leek soup, 88–89
Potato pancakes, crisp, 83–84
Potato salad
    American, 139
    German, 140
Potatoes, and celery root, purée of, 117
Potatoes, French roast, 133
Potatoes, gratin, 104
Potatoes, mashed, 121
Potted shrimp, 132–133
Preparations, 1–11
Prunes in Madiera, 127
Pudding, Coach House plum, 10–11

Pudding, Yorkshire, 117
Puff pastry, 30–32
  choux, chicken livers and mushrooms in, 89–90
  mushroom-filled, 106–107
Punch, champagne, 69

Q

Quince, roast ducks with, 123–124

R

Rabbit braised in red wine, 82
Ratatouille, egg cake, 92–94
Red cabbage, 128
Relish, cranberry-orange-nut, 120
Relish tray, 138
Remoulade, celery, 81
Rice, boiled, 78
Rice pilaf, 108
Roast ducks with quince, 123–124
Roast fresh ham, 139
Roast goose with pears and prunes, 126–127
Roast potatoes, French, 133
Roasted pecans, 64
Roulade, finnan haddie, with mustard sauce, 97–98
Royal icing, 24
Rum, hot buttered, 71

S

St. Nicholas spice cookies, 23
Salad(s)
  beet and onion, 141
  cole slaw, 141
  endive, 99
  fruit and onion, 158
  mixed green, with garlic-flavored vinaigrette, 79
  potato
    American, 140
    German, 139
Salad dressing, garlic-flavored vinaigrette, 79
Salmon, smoked, 64
Sauce
  Cranberry, 120
  Hard, 11
  Mignonette, 62
  Mustard dill, 144
  for roast ducks with quince, 123

Sausage, cotechino, 151
Sausage stuffing, 119
Sautéed snow peas, 103
Scotch black bun, 8–9
Shell roast of beef, 133
Sheraton, Mimi, 23
Shirred eggs, 111
Shrimp, curried, 76–78
Shrimp, pickled, 62
Shrimp, potted, 132–133
Shrimp with cucumber boats, 67
Smoked salmon–cheese spread, 64
Soufflé, cold lime, 80
Soups
  consommé
    Bellevue, 92
    with marrow balls, 125–126
  Old-fashioned vegetable-beef, 145
  potato and leek, 88–89
Spaetzle, 128
Spice cookies
  Christmas trees, 16
  mushroom, 17
  St. Nicholas, 23
Spiced Christmas trees, 16
Spiced mushroom cookies, 17
Spinach, creamed, 83
Springerle, 24–25
Spritz cookies, 19
Standing rib roast of beef, 116
Stanish, Rudolf, 78
Star of Zurich, 48–49
Stocking stuffers, 55–60
Stollen, 44–45
Strawberry cream roll, 105
Stuffing, sausage, 119
Swedish hash, 113

T

Tart, open-faced apple, 95
Tartletts, mincemeat, 34–35
Template, star, 49
Toddy, hot, 71
Tom and Jerry, 70
Tomatoes, cherry, with basil, 134
Topping, from German butter cake, 52–53
Trifle, 135–136

Truffles, chocolate, 137
Turkey, roast, with sausage stuffing, 118–119
Turkey of the farm, 102
Turnip-crabmeat canapés, 63
Turnips, mashed yellow, 120

V

Vegetable-beef soup, old-fashioned, 145
Vinaigrette, garlic-flavored, 79

W

Walnut balls, 20
Walnut cake, 39–40

Walnut marzipan, 40
Wasps' nests, 16
Wassail, 70
White, Donald Bruce, 63
White bread, 46
Whole wheat bread, 47
Williams, Dennis, 70
Wine, 76
  rabbit braised in, 82
Wine jelly, 129
Wright, Elizabeth, 129

Y

Yorkshire pudding, 117
Youngerman, Genevieve, 55